VEDANTA PHILOSOPHY

VEDANTA PHILOSOPHY

Divine Heritage of Man

BY

SWAMI ABHEDANANDA

GYAN

Published by

GYAN

Gyan Publishing House
5, Ansari Road
Daryaganj, New Delhi-110002
Phone: 011-47034999, 9811692060
E-mail: books@gyanbooks.com

Distribution Network
gyanbooks.com
India, USA, Canada, UK, Australia, France

ISBN : 978-81-212-2156-6 (PB)
First Published, 1903

2nd Impression 2021

Printed at: Gyan Press, Delhi.

Vedanta Philosophy
Author: Swami Abhedananda

VEDÄNTA PHILOSOPHY

Divine Heritage of Man

BY

SWÂMI ABHEDÂNANDA

PUBLISHED BY

THE VEDÂNTA SOCIETY

NEW YORK

Dedicated

to the

Beloved and Revered Memory

of the

BLESSED SWÂMI VIVEKÂNANDA

My Spiritual Brother and

Fellow Disciple of

BHAGAVÂN SRÎ RÂMAKRISHNA

Contents.

Existence of God.

"That which exists is one: men call it by various names."—Rig veda, I, 164, 46.

The Existence of God.

HUMAN minds seem to have almost exhausted their reasoning powers in producing all kinds of arguments that can be given both for and against the existence of God. For hundreds of years philosophers, scientists, and theologians among all nations have been bringing forward proofs either to show that there is such a Being as God or to deny His existence entirely. Of course most of the arguments and proofs in favor of the existence of God are convincing to those who already have some sort of belief in the Creator or some conception of the Supreme Being. If we have been brought up in an atmosphere where there prevails a belief in God as the Creator and Ruler of the universe or as an extra-mundane Being who, dwelling outside of nature, commands everything and directs the movements of the world, then unconsciously we breathe in and imbibe that belief from our childhood, and as we grow older we accept all the arguments and evidences that we can find in support of this preconceived idea.

If we have already a conception of God as the First Cause, then all the inductions and inferences which maintain that idea will naturally appeal to us and we shall take them for granted. But those whose minds are not biased or influenced by any such idea, belief, or conception, those who are able to examine these proofs critically in the light of modern science, applying logic and reason, and those who freely investigate nature, searching for an extra-cosmic creator and ruler of the universe, may fail to find any convincing proof, and may therefore deny the existence of God, as such, or as the First Cause of all.

We all know how the theory of evolution has revolutionized the old idea of the special creation of the world out of nothing at some definite period of time. Those who found consolation in the design theory and held it to be the most unassailable ground in favor of the existence of an Omnipotent Designer, are now hopelessly discouraged by the introduction of the Darwinian theories of natural selection and sexual selection. By these theories we can explain almost all the so-called designs of the Creator. Moreover, the design argument cannot make clear why under the government of a just, omnipotent, and omniscient Ruler should happen such disorders as the volcanic eruptions on the Island of Martinique, or as the plagues, famines, and other disasters which devastate different countries, destroying hundreds of thousands of innocent living creatures. The design theory cannot trace the causes of such disasters; for if there were a Designer, His design should be perfect and there should be harmony instead of discord.

The monotheistic religions have tried to explain the cause of all the disorders that occur in the universe by a theory of a Creator of evil as distinct and separate from the Designer of good. This method of explanation, however, does not help us much in proving the existence of a perfect, all-powerful and infinite God, for we shall then have to admit two beings, one the creator of good and the other the creator of evil, which will make each limited by the other and will take away all idea of the omnipotency and infinity of the Supreme Being.

Those who believe that God is the First Cause of the universe, must determine the nature of that first cause—whether He is the efficient or the material cause. We know that these two causes are essential for the production of a thing, as, in the case of a pot, the potter is the efficient and the earth is the material cause. Now if we say that God is the efficient or instrumental cause of the universe, like the maker of a pot, then it would have been impossible for Him to create without the help of the material cause, which must have coexisted with the Creator. Here we are confronted with the same difficulty—that God who stands outside the material cause, is limited by matter, therefore He cannot be unlimited in the proper sense of the term. If, on the contrary, the material cause be meant by First Cause, then He must have gone through all the changes of evolution, which would make Him like a changeable, phenomenal object of the universe, a conclusion which we cannot accept.

The moral argument that the moral laws presuppose a law-giver cannot prove the existence of God, since we know that natural laws do not presuppose a law-giver. In the first place we should understand what "law" means. The forces of nature are operating in the universe in certain modes, and when the regularity and uniformity of these modes are observed and interpreted by the human mind, they are called "laws"; consequently these laws are to be found neither in nature nor outside of it, but in the human mind. Secondly, as in external nature the natural forces acting under regular modes do not presuppose a law-giver, so it can be shown that the moral laws are but modes in which natural forces operate on the moral plane; that they do not need a moral law-giver, but their process is the same as the evolutionary process of the physical world. Furthermore, all such conceptions of God as the natural law-giver or the moral law-giver are rejected by advanced thinkers as the anthropomorphic ideas of uncultured minds.

All these proofs and many other arguments like these which were considered to be sufficient to establish the existence of an extra-cosmic creator, ruler, or law-giver of the universe, are now thrown aside as imperfect and fallacious. In these days of science and reason when we try to prove the existence of God, we do not search for a creator or fashioner of the world, for a designer or first cause of the phenomenal universe; neither do we look for a moral law-giver; our conception of God has outgrown those stages of evolution and has become as large as the infinity of the universe. We no longer think that this earth is the stationary centre around which the sun, moon and other luminaries of the heavens revolve, moved by the supernatural power of angels, who, according to the old-fashioned belief, dwelt above the blue dome of the sky overhead and moved these planets according to their whims and fancies. We are just beginning to understand the vastness of the universe. Modern astronomy has opened our eyes to the fact that this earth which we inhabit is to be considered as an infinitesimal point when compared with the immensity of space and with the innumerable cosmic bodies that exist above the horizon. We have learned that there are heavenly bodies beyond our solar system, the nearest one of which is so distant from us that its light, travelling at the rate of one hundred and eighty-six thousand miles per second, requires three and a half years to reach our earth. There are other stars so remote that thousands of years are needed for their light, travelling at the same rate, to arrive at our planet. We are assured that more than one thousand million stars have been discovered by the telescope and that there may be millions and millions of suns which are yet beyond the reach of our best instruments.

Thus, as far as we can get by stretching our imagination we do not find any limit or boundary to the universe; we still have the feeling that there is something beyond. This sense of something existing beyond what we know and perceive is always with us; we cannot get rid of it. Even when we try to perceive a finite object, that sense of beyond is most intimately connected with our perception and conception of it. There is a feeling of the infinite very closely associated with all our ideas and concepts. Take, for instance, the geometrical figure, a square; when we try to perceive that square, we can only perceive it by perceiving the space beyond it. We see it as a figure enclosed by four straight lines, but at the same time there is a feeling of the space beyond, otherwise we could not perceive the square.

Again when we look at the space which is circumscribed by the horizon we do not lose the sense that there is something beyond that limit, that infinite space extends beyond the visible horizon. The same perception of limitlessness or of the infinite is closely associated with the idea of time. We cannot conceive either its beginning or its end. There always remains the sense of the eternal beyond both before and after our conception of time. In this way we get the perception of eternity. The human mind is so peculiarly constituted that it is incapable of finding the absolutely defined limit of any thing of the world. Trees, mountains, rivers, earth, sun, moon, and all other objects of the senses are tangible, but do we find any definite limit when we carefully analyze our perceptions of these objects? No, we do not. We may try our best, but we are sure to discover, sooner or later, that there is a sense of beyond constantly attached to them.

Let us take an illustration: suppose that we stand under a big oak tree; we may look at it, touch it, or smell it, but can we perceive the absolute limit of that tree? Do our senses take in the whole tree at one time? No, our senses cannot reach its deepest roots or its highest branches, nor do we know what is going on under the bark or in the leaves. It is impossible for any one to take in the whole tree at one time; we may take it in by parts, but at the same time the perception of each part will under all circumstances leave in our minds the sense of beyond. Again when we think of the innumerable atoms and molecules that make up the body of that tree, its finite form vanishes, leaving an impression that what we call "tree" is indeed an expression of the infinite; for when the form is gone, that which is left of the tree is inseparable from the infinite ocean of some substance imperceptible to the senses. Moreover, when we try to know the power or force that gives form to that tree and makes it living, which cannot be separated from it, then in one sense we must say that the tree has in it something intangible, mysterious and unknowable; we cannot help it.

In the same manner it can be shown that every finite perception or conception of an object brings with it a sense of beyond, a perception of the infinite, or something that is unknown and unknowable, of something that is eternal. Take a drop of water which is finite; put it under the microscope and you will see infinitesimal atoms moving about, some clearly visible, some so minute that they are hardly perceptible with the help of the most powerful microscope. Yet modern chemistry tells us that we can ascertain the relative position of these atoms so minute that millions upon millions of them could stand upon the point of a needle. Is not the infinitude of this small drop of water as wonderful as the infinity of space? Indeed the drop of water is finite and infinite at the same time. When we see a flower, or touch it, we cannot help realizing in the same way that it is the finite appearance of that something which we cannot know, which is infinite and eternal. It is like a beautiful painting upon the canvas of that eternal invisible substance of the universe which the senses cannot perceive, which the mind cannot grasp or comprehend; it is the expression of that infinite matter which fills all space. No one can deny the existence of this substance which appears to our senses in an infinite variety of forms and shapes.

Modern science tells us that this all-pervading substance of the universe has neither beginning nor end, because we cannot know its limit either in space or in time. As far back as we can go in our conception of time, we find that the sense of beyond is present; it is therefore eternal, that is, beginningless and endless. It is neither increased nor diminished by anything; we cannot add one iota to this substance, nor can we subtract anything from it; it is consequently unchangeable in quantity as well as in quality. It is all-powerful because all the forces manifested in the perceptible world proceed from and rest upon that unlimited substance. We may call it by whatever name we like; it is the real essence of all phenomena. It is like the ocean upon which the waves of phenomenal forms are rising and, after playing their parts, are disappearing again and again. All these forms of sun, or moon, or stars, of human beings or animals, are nothing but waves in that infinite ocean. As the waves cannot exist without the ocean, so finite objects cannot exist without the infinite substance which is behind and beyond all phenomena. That infinite substance is the support of the universe; it is one because it is infinite; if the infinite were many, it would lose its limitless nature and become finite.

Ever since the dawn of intellect upon the horizon of the human mind there has been a constant struggle for a definite knowledge of this something which is beyond all finite existence and yet is not finite. The human mind cannot rest contented with the mere play of appearances, but always yearns to know what it is that appears. From ancient times those who have had some kind of perception of this infinite as related to the phenomenal universe have also tried to express their ideas by giving different names to it. Thus have arisen the various names by which human minds have designated this infinite substance; but each of these names now stands like a landmark in the path of the evolution of the conception of God. Whether we call that infinite substance God, or Creator, or Designer, or First Cause, or the Father, or Jehovah, or Allah, or Brahman, we mean the same infinite, eternal, all-powerful and unchangeable Substance. Every individual has a vague perception of this infinite around him or her; some are more conscious of it than others. The more that we are dissatisfied and discontented with finite things, the stronger grows in us the desire to know more about this infinite, to understand more about that something which is not finite, which is beyond finite time and beyond limited space. When we find no pleasure, no satisfaction, no happiness in objects limited by time and space, and when we realize the transitoriness of all that is finite, our inner nature longs for that which is absolutely unlimited, and we wish to know where it is and how it is. We seek it here and there, not knowing exactly what we want; we struggle for knowledge; and this struggle, this search for that Infinite Being, grows stronger and stronger until the realization of the true nature of the infinite is obtained.

To a materialist who studies the objective side of the universe, this infinite substance appears as material and insentient; he calls it matter, and tries to deduce this phenomenal world from this infinite unintelligent matter. The matter of the materialist, however, is as infinite, as eternal, as all-powerful as the God or the Supreme Being of the religionists. A materialist simply studies the objective world and does not recognize or study the subjective universe; therefore he is satisfied with his conclusions; but as the objective side is only one-half of the universe, his conclusions are one-sided. Those who, on the contrary, study subjective nature, discover the same infinite behind their limited minds, beyond every idea, thought, feeling, or sensation. The finite mind is that which takes the forms of thoughts, ideas, feelings, sensations, and which is limited by the sense of "I." When, however, we try to think of the definite boundary of the sense of "I" or of the finite mind, we cannot find it; we fail to trace the beginning or end of that which thinks, or feels, or perceives, or conceives, or imagines. We realize that as physical forms are like the waves in the infinite ocean of eternal space filled with substance, so thoughts, ideas, feelings, sensations are but so many waves in the infinite ocean of mental space filled with finer substance. As we cannot attach the sense of "I" to our physical form, so we cannot call these mental forms our own. Thus after careful study the students of the subjective world come to the conclusion that the subjective infinite is the Reality of the universe, and that external phenomena are but the representations or projections of the subjective infinite, or mind. According to them time and space do not exist outside the mind, consequently everything in space and time is like a picture of the subjective idea. They deny the existence of matter and trace the origin of all qualities or powers of the finite mind to that infinite mind. They give the attribute of intelligence to it and call it the eternal, intelligent, cosmic mind. The existence of infinite mind is as undeniable as that of infinite matter. But this substance, whether we call it mind or matter, subject or object, is the one unknowable Being of the universe. All mental as well as all physical forms are but its appearances. It is called in Sanskrit *Brahman*. From this infinite and eternal Brahman we have come into existence; in It we live and into It we return at the end of phenomenal existence.

In ancient India the question was asked, "What is God?" The answer we find in Vedanta: "That from which all animate and inanimate objects have come into existence, in which they live and play like waves in the sea, and into which they return ultimately at the time of dissolution, know that to be Brahman, or the infinite Substance, or God." Who can live without being sustained by this Infinite One? As a painting cannot stand without the background, so phenomena cannot exist without being supported by the infinite Substance or Brahman. It pervades the universe, interpenetrating atoms and molecules, yet it lies beyond all the mental and physical phenomena of the manifested universe. It is not confined by the limitations of sex or gender; we may call this Being he, she, or it. This infinite substance or Brahman is incomprehensible and unknowable to finite minds. That to which the modern agnostics refer when they use the term "Unknowable" is the same Infinite Being.

Here we must not forget the meaning of the verb "to know." In its ordinary sense "to know" means first to perceive through the senses and then to form a concept of the object perceived. Consequently, all our knowledge is limited by the power of perception as well as by the mind. To know God or the Infinite

Being by the same kind of knowledge as that by which we know a stone or a tree or a dog would be tantamount to annihilating God. Because a known God in this sense would cease to be God; He would become a phenomenal object, an idol, and not the Infinite Being, for in trying to know God, we would be bringing that Infinite Being within the limits of our finite mind. In this sense, therefore, God, or the Infinite Being, is always unknown and unknowable. Shall we then join the agnostics and be contented with our ignorance and powerlessness to know the Infinite? Shall we cease from all our attempts and struggles to understand the nature of the Infinite or to know the existence of God when He is unknowable? No. Here is a great fact to learn, that although the Infinite Being is unknown and unknowable according to the point of view of modern agnosticism, He is more than known, more than knowable from the standpoint of the Vedanta. He is the essence of our being, the essence of our Self. He is the source of our knowledge. All knowledge proceeds from that infinite Wisdom; when we know a thing, we know it in and through Him. When, for instance, we know a table, we say that the table is known, but can we trace the source of this knowledge? Do we know from where it comes? It is not created by us. It is eternal; it exists in the infinite mind or that something behind the finite mind, and through that knowledge we say that the table is known. When we say that ether is unknown and unknowable, we use this same knowledge as our guide. That by which we are able to cognize a thing and to call it known or unknown is Divinity itself. Therefore whether we know a thing or do not know it, knowledge in either case is possible only through the one source of all wisdom and consciousness.

It is for this reason that God is more than anything known and knowable or anything unknown and unknowable. He is infinitely higher than either. He is the essence of the ego or "I"; no one can live without being sustained by that infinite source of existence, knowledge, and consciousness. It is not that God dwells somewhere outside of the universe and from there is making my blood circulate or my heart beat, but He is in every cell of my body. He fills the space of my form. I owe my existence to Him. He is the Soul of my soul as well as the Soul of the universe. He is in you, in me, in the chair, in the wall and everywhere, yet we do not see or know Him. It would be a great degradation of God if He could be known by our ordinary knowledge. He would then be like a changeable, limited, phenomenal something such as we perceive with our senses; whereas He is in fact the Knower of the universe, the Eternal Subject who knows everything in each of us. The Knower or the Subject in us is unchangeable, eternal and one.

When we understand that by knowledge is meant objectification, we realize that all our attempts to express that infinite Subject in language—to call Him Father, Brother, or dearest Friend—are nothing but so many efforts of the human mind to objectify the infinite, unlimited Subject of the universe. We cannot, however, remain satisfied with this imperfect knowledge of Divinity; we desire to know more about the Infinite Being. Gradually we may come to realize that He is the Creator of the world, the Governor of all, or the First Cause of the universe. But here again we shall not rest content; we shall still wish to know more about Him. Then we shall find that the same Infinite Substance or Being which is beyond every finite object, beyond space and time, above mind and body, is in reality not very far from us; wherefore it is said in the Vedanta:

"He is far from us, yet He is nearer than the nearest; He dwells in everything, yet He is outside the phenomenal universe; He is infinitely smaller than the atom of an atom, yet He is infinitely larger than the largest solar system, than the space which covers the perceptible universe."

The Existence of God.

When we see the sun, moon, or stars, we see that part of the Infinite which is visible to our eyes; when we hear a sound, we perceive that part of the Infinite which is audible to our ears; but God is in reality beyond light, sound, odor, taste or touch. He is the same Infinite Substance which transcends time and space, mind and sense powers. By knowing so much of the Infinite, however, we are yet unsatisfied, we still desire to know more. Our souls still long for a deeper knowledge of that all-pervading Substance. The more we study phenomenal objects the less are we content with the knowledge that we can gather from this study. We may devote the whole of our lives and spend all the energy we possess in trying to satisfy this craving for knowledge of the Infinite by studying the phenomenal world, but this thirst for knowledge will not be quenched; it will remain, as it does in all the great thinkers of the world. We may read books, philosophies, sciences, and Scriptures, but the longing of the soul will never be fulfilled by reading books. There is only one way to quench this thirst and that is by realizing the Infinite.

The word "realize" means something more than ordinary knowing. By "realizing" we mean being and becoming one with the Infinite. If we can know that the all-pervading Being is the Essence of our lives and the Soul of our souls, we become more and more acquainted with that Infinite and understand its whole nature—not the objective side alone, not merely as the material substance, but as the infinite mind substance, and also as that which transcends this substance of mental phenomena. I mean when we have realized the Infinite Spirit, when we have found that It is the source of all powers and forces as well as the basis of our consciousness, the foundation of our existence, the life and the reality of the universe, then the thirst for knowledge is quenched, then all questions regarding the existence of God are answered, all doubts cease forever.

But it may be asked: How can we know the Supreme Being as the Soul of our souls? By rising above the plane of consciousness of the finite. This plane of consciousness will never reveal the true nature of the Infinite Being because it functions within the limitations of the senses, consequently it cannot reach the infinite which is above all limits. We may have a vague perception of it or we may think of it as the subject or object, as mind or matter; but that is not the same as the realization of the Absolute One. If we can rise above time and space, shutting out all sense objects, making the mind impervious to all sensations of external objects, if we can then direct the whole energy of mind and soul towards the Infinite within us, then we shall be able to realize the Soul of our souls, then the truth of the existence of God will be revealed to us.

If we wish to know God, we shall have to enter into the state of superconsciousness. All the great spiritual leaders of the world, Jesus the Christ, Buddha, Râmakrishna, and others, who preached the existence of God, first realized Him by entering into the state of superconsciousness. Those who have studied Raja Yoga* and have practised it will understand what superconsciousness means. All revelation and inspiration come in that state. The longing for more knowledge has led the river of the soul into the ocean of Infinite Wisdom. In that state the individual soul realizes the blissfulness which is beyond the reach of ordinary mortals, which cannot be obtained by wealth, property, or worldly prosperity. Friends and relatives cannot help us in rising to that blissful condition. It is a state attaining which nothing remains unattainable, realizing which the true nature of everything is revealed. It is a state in which no desire remains unfulfilled, in which the individual soul, transcending all limitations, becomes one with the Infinite and enjoys un-

* "Râja Yoga," by Swami Vivekananda. Published under the auspices of the Vedanta Society of New York.

bounded happiness both here and hereafter. Such a knower of the Infinite says:

"I have attained everything that is to be attained, I have realized all that can be realized. I have known that Infinite Being that is worshipped under different names by different nations as God, or Father in heaven, or Allah, or Buddha, or Christ, or Divine Mother, or Brahman."

Attributes of God.

"The Supreme Spirit is devoid of the defining attributes of form, color, etc. He is unchangeable, unborn, eternal, indestructible, imperishable and is always of one nature. He is pure and the repository of all blessed qualities."
—Vishnu Purana.

Attributes of God.

God is described in the different Scriptures as a spirit, infinite, eternal, unchangeable, true and one; the omnipotent and omniscient creator and governor of the universe, and the repository of all blessed qualities, such as justice, goodness, mercy, and love. If we ask a Christian, a Jew, a Mahometan, a Parsee, a Hindu, or a follower of any other sect or creed what is his conception of God, each one of them will quote passages from his Scriptures giving the same attributes to the Divine Being, whom they worship under various names—such as Father in heaven, Jehovah, Allah, Ahura Mazda, or Brahman. The names may vary but the attributes of God are with each exactly the same.

A catholic priest who bows down before the

image of Jesus the Christ and prays to Him, who burns incense and lights candles; a protestant clergyman who does not believe in bowing down before any image; a Mahometan priest who is a fanatical iconoclast and denies all forms of God; or a Hindu priest who worships an idol in a temple, invariably agree with one another in describing the attributes of the God they worship. There is no difference between the God of a Christian or a Mahometan of a Parsee or a Hindu, because each of them believes that God is infinite and one.

How can there be many Gods when their attributes are the same and identical everywhere? Yet a Christian calls the Hindu a heathen, and a Mahometan calls a Christian an unbeliever, and each in turn quarrels with the other. Why is there so much persecution if God is one? Because of the ignorance of His believers. They do not even try to understand the true meaning of any of the attributes which they give to God; their eyes are blinded by ignorance, fanaticism and bigotry. Stimulated by false belief and superstition, they maintain that their God is the only true God, while the God of other nations is untrue, and they cannot see that every one worships the same Infinite Being. Fanatical Christians preach: "Beware of the God of the heathen, He cannot give salvation to His worshippers"; as if there were *two* Gods.

Ignorance is the mother of fanaticism, bigotry, superstition, and of all that springs from them. Fanatics cannot realize that God is the common property of all, that whether He be worshipped by a Christian or by a Hindu, He is one, because His attributes are identical. Among those who are not so fanatical there are many who give the same attributes to God without, however, understanding their true meaning. Ninety per cent. of monotheists all over the world say: "God is infinite and one," but at the same time they think of some being with a human form sitting somewhere outside of the universe. If we ask them the meaning of the word "infinite," their answers are often full of illogical nonsense. They will make God as finite as possible and bring forward all sorts of fallacious arguments to support their position.

Those who believe in a personal God, give Him a human form, human attributes and a human personality without realizing that they are making their Lord limited in power, personality and attributes. Of course it is not their fault; it is quite natural that they should think of the Ruler of the universe as a human being, because we are all human and the limit of our conception is a human being. Our world is a human world, our God must be a human God, and our explanation of the universe must also be human. Having seen the governor of a country, who is a human being with certain powers, we form a concept and keep it in our minds when we conceive the Supreme Being as the governor of the universe. Naturally we give Him a human form and a human personality, only with this difference—that the governor of the country is limited in power, size, and qualifications, while the Ruler of the universe is unlimited in power and immensely magnified in size and qualifications; yet however great He may be, He must still appear more or less like a human being. In this way our explanation of the universe has become human, and our God has acquired a human form and personality. If a cow became a philosopher and had a religion, her conception of God would be in cow form, her explanation of the universe would be through that cow God. She would not be able to comprehend our Lord at all. Similarly if a tiger had a God, his conception would be of a tiger form. If there be a being with a form different from ours, with a nature higher than ours, his God will be like himself. As we do not know what conception of God the people of Mars have, we cannot know their God; if they are not like human beings, their conception will differ from ours. So none of these pictures of God and none of these explanations of the universe can be complete in itself. It may be a partial truth, but not the whole truth. Therefore all those conceptions of God which we so often hear—that He is like a human being sitting on a throne outside the universe and from there governing the universe by His powers, are incomplete and imperfect.

But ordinary people do not see this. Each is sure that his conception and explanation are the best. They cannot realize how there can be anything higher or greater than what they already believe. Yet when they are asked, what are the attributes of such a human God, they will say: "He is a spirit, infinite, eternal, unchangeable, true and one; He is the omniscient and omnipotent creator and the repository of all blessed qualities." Thus they unconsciously make God finite and infinite at the same time. Can there be anything more absurd and self-contradictory than a finite infinite God! If He is finite, He is limited by time, space and causation, must have a beginning and end, and cannot be unchangeable. A finite God must be changeable and must perish like all mortal things. Are we ready to believe in such a perishable God? Not for a moment. We cannot give any form to God because form means limitation in space by time. By giving a form to God, we make Him subject to time, space and the law of causation, consequently we make Him mortal like any other object of the phenomenal universe which has form. God with a form cannot be immortal and eternal, He must die. Therefore we cannot say that God is finite or that He has any form.

He is infinite. But let us have a clear understanding of the meaning of this word "infinite," and use it in its proper sense. That which is not limited by time and space and not subject to the law of causation, which is above time, space, and beyond all laws is infinite. God is not limited by time or space, neither has He any cause. He is absolute. The infinite again must be one, otherwise it is finite. If there be any other thing beside that infinite then it is no longer infinite; it is limited by that object, consequently it has become finite. Thus if we admit that God is infinite, we deny the existence of any other thing besides God; otherwise He would be limited by that thing, and be subject to time, space and the law of causation.

If we say that matter exists separate from and outside of God, we have made Him limited by matter, we have made Him finite and perishable. If we think of ourselves as separate from God, as independent of His Being, then in our thought we have denied His illimitable nature. There is for the same reason, not a single particle of matter in the universe that can exist independent of God's existence or outside of God; if He is infinite and one, our bodies and every thing of the universe from the minutest atom to the largest planetary system, from the lowest animalcule to the highest Being, exists in and through that Infinite Existence. This may be startling to many, but the fact cannot be denied. If we wish to be logical, if the word "infinite" conveys any meaning at all, we cannot avoid the logical conclusion which must inevitably follow. If, on the contrary, we use the word "infinite" meaning something finite, how foolish and illogical shall we be! The conclusion is this: If God is infinite and one, then mind and matter, subject and object, creator and creation, and all relative dual existences are within that Being, and not outside of it. The whole universe is in God and God is in it; it is inseparable from God. I am in Him and He is in me; each one of us is inseparable from His being; if one atom of my body exists, that existence cannot be separated from His existence.

We have now understood the meaning of the two attributes infinite and one. Let us examine the meaning of other attributes. God is unchangeable, that is, He is always the same and never subject to any change whatsoever, because He is eternal, without beginning or end. That which has a beginning must have an end and go through all the changes of birth, growth, decay and death; everything that has a beginning must grow, decay and die. That which is limited by time and space must go through all these changes, which, on the contrary, never affect the infinite Being.

God is a spirit. What is to be understood by spirit? It does not mean a shadowy form or an apparition. By this term is meant pure, self-luminous intelligence, the source of all consciousness, the basis and foundation of all knowledge, the background of mind and matter, of subject and object. Again He is true. That which is not God is untrue or unreal; or, in other words, that which is finite, manifold, changeable, non-eternal, transitory, is untrue and unreal. Furthermore, God is omnipresent and omniscient, and upon Him depends the existence of mind and matter, of subject and object. Let us understand this a little more clearly. Whatever exists in the universe, whether mental or physical, subjective or objective, can exist only as related to a self-conscious intelligence. When we analyze our perceptions, we find that that which is not related to any state of our consciousness does not exist in relation to us, because we do not know anything about it. Existence and knowledge or consciousness are inseparable.

As our small worlds of which we are conscious, exist in relation to our conscious being, so the phenomenal universe can only exist as being related to the knowledge of the cosmic knower or the universal Being; otherwise there cannot be any existence, because existence and knowledge, existence and consciousness are inseparable; therefore God is called omniscient or all-knowing. Nothing exists without being related directly to the intelligence and knowledge of the infinite Being. As this infinite Being pervades the universe and interpenetrates every particle of matter, giving existence to everything, so the light of His knowledge pervades the universe; therefore He is omnipresent and omniscient. If these various conceptions, obtained by analyzing the attributes of God, be summed up, we shall learn that God is the Absolute Being, eternal, true and everlasting, the one infinite ocean of self-existent, self-luminous intelligence which is the source of all consciousness. Nothing can exist outside of or independent of that one omnipresent and omniscient Being of the universe.

Here a question arises,—if there be no other being beside God, what will become of the diverse phenomena of the universe, which we perceive with our senses? Do they not exist? Yes, they do, but their existence depends upon God. They have no separate and independent existence; they are like froth, bubbles and waves on that infinite ocean of intelligence. As a wave cannot exist for a moment independent of the ocean, so the phenomena of the world depend for their existence upon the Absolute Being.

This ocean of pure self-luminous intelligence and existence is described in Vedanta by the word *Brahman*, which means absolute existence and intelligence, the unlimited source of knowledge and of consciousness; while the power which produces these waves of phenomena is called *Mâyâ*. This inscrutable power of *Mâyâ* dwells in the infinite ocean of Reality or Brahman from eternity to eternity. It is as inseparable from the Divine Being as the power of burning is inseparable from fire. Sometimes this power remains latent as undifferentiated cosmic energy and sometimes it manifests itself as the various forces of nature. When that power is latent, all phenomena disappear, and dissolution or involution takes place; but when it begins to express itself as natural forces, it produces the waves and bubbles of phenomena in the ocean of Brahman. Then the Absolute Being seen through the active or manifesting power of *Mâyâ* or cosmic energy, appears as the creator and governor of the universe.

He is called in Sanskrit "Iswara," which means also the creator and ruler of the universe. He is the first-born lord, or the cosmic ego. This cosmic ego, the Iswara or lord, is called the creator of the universe. Here let us understand clearly in what sense God can be properly called the creator of the world. Does He create it out of nothing as described in the monotheistic and dualistic Scriptures of the Christians, Jews, Mahometans, and Parsees? No, He does not create anything out of nothing; He is not the creator in that sense. In the first place we must not forget the truth, discovered and established by ancient and modern science, that something cannot come out of nothing, consequently to a scientific mind creation out of nothing has no meaning. The theory of a special creation of the world as we read in Genesis has been proved to be an unscientific myth. Secondly, the doctrine of evolution is now so unquestionably established that we can safely accept it in the place of the mythical story of special creation. Therefore when we speak of God as the creator of the universe, we do not mean one who brought the world into existence out of nothing as our forefathers understood by this expression; but applying the light of science and being guided by the reasoning of the Vedanta philosophy, we must understand that Iswara is called the creator because He projects out of His own being the powers existing there potentially and makes them active. Thus the word creator means the projector of all forces and of all phenomenal forms which potentially existed as eternal energy in Iswara. That projection from the potential into the kinetic or active state takes place gradually through the process of the evolution of the Mâyâ or the cosmic energy which dwells in the Iswara of Vedanta. Vedanta teaches that although Brahman or the

Absolute Being or Godhead is above all activity, still the Iswara is full of power and action. He starts the evolution of the cosmic energy which before the beginning of the cyclic evolution held all phenomenal names and forms in its bosom. Iswara, according to Vedanta, is both the material and the efficient cause of the universe. He does not create matter, but matter is only a certain state or mode of motion of the universal Divine energy. When the dormant power of Mâyâ begins to manifest, all material forms commence to appear.

The next attribute of Iswara is that of ruler or governor of the universe. How does He govern? Does He govern the world from outside, as it is said in the Christian Scriptures? No, He governs from within and never from without. He is the *Antar-yâmin*, the internal ruler of the universe. As the soul is the internal ruler of the body, so Iswara, being the soul of the universe, governs it from within and not from outside.

Attributes of God.

He is the repository of all blessed qualities, that is, all that is good, all that is great, all that is sublime, is but the expression of the Divine power. But God Himself is above good and evil, beyond virtue and vice, above all relativity and beyond all conditions. He loves all beings equally and impartially; He does not love one nation for certain qualifications and hate other nations, but He loves every living soul, whether human or animal, equally. Just as the sun shines alike upon the heads of sages and sinners, so the love of that Divine Being touches the souls of all. Why does He love all beings equally? Because each individual soul is related to God as a part is related to the whole. As a part cannot exist independently, so our souls cannot exist independent of the Soul of the universe. Therefore we live and move and exist in and through the whole, or Iswara. God loves His parts because He cannot help it. How can it be otherwise? How is it possible for a whole not to love its own parts? Love means the expression of oneness. At the bottom of all earthly love exists this idea of oneness; the lover and the beloved must be one, one in spirit, in thoughts, in ideas, in everything, otherwise there is no real love. Therefore God is all-loving. Thus if we try with the aid of the light of science and reason to understand the true significance of the attributes of God, we are forcibly driven to the conclusions of Vedanta. With the help of Vedanta we can realize the true relation which the universe bears to God, which the individual soul bears to the infinite Being.

If we once understand that God is the source of all existence and power and is the one Reality, that outside of God no existence is possible, then we begin to feel the presence of divinity everywhere. In every action of our lives we realize that the divine power is working through us, and at every moment of our earthly existence we feel ourselves to be like so many instruments through which the Divine will is manifesting itself and doing whatever He ordains. All the actions of our lives are then turned into acts of worship of the Supreme Deity. Being dead to selfishness, we are then able to say from the bottom of our hearts, "O Lord, Thy will, not mine, be done."

All fear then vanishes, all sins are redeemed, and the individual soul becomes free from the bondage of ignorance and selfishness. This realization leads to a still higher and closer union with the Divine. The soul gradually realizes spiritual oneness with the universal Spirit or Brahman. Thus having attained to God-consciousness, which is the highest ideal of all religions, the individual soul becomes like Christ and declares "I and my Father are one."

Has God any Form?

"The all-pervading, omnipotent and formless Spirit manifests Himself in various forms under different names to fulfil the desires of His worshippers."—Vishnu Purana.

Has God any Form?

STUDENTS of the Old Testament are familiar with the fact that the ancient Israelites conceived their God Elohim or Yahveh, the Lord God, as possessing human attributes and a human form. There are many passages which testify that God walked with Adam and Eve and spoke to them; He ate and drank with the elders of Israel; and the Lord said to Moses: "I will cover thee with my hand while I pass by, and I will take my hand away and thou shalt see my back parts; but my face shalt not be seen." (Ex. xxxiii, 22, 23.) Yahveh was the Lord of the House of Israel. He was, moreover, not only the God of Abraham and of Moses, but He became the Supreme Being and the only God, above all gods. Upon this conception of the Supreme

Being with a human form and human personality have been built the structures of the two great monotheistic or dualistic religions, Judaism and Christianity.

The same Elohim or Yahveh, the Lord of the house of Israel, the God of Abraham, of Isaac and Jacob, and of Moses, is the almighty Creator, Ruler, and Father in heaven of the Jews and Christians of the present day. He sits on a throne outside the universe, having a right hand and a left hand, and according to the Christian belief, Jesus sits at His right hand. Neither Christ nor Moses nor any of the prophets had to introduce a new God among the Jews. All of them accepted and worshipped the same Elohim or Yahveh, who was at first only the tribal god of the house of Israel. Here we must not forget the original meaning of the word "Elohim," which, although translated into English in the Old Testament as God, at first meant "that which is feared" and was sometimes used vaguely to describe unseen powers or "objects of man's fear" or superhuman beings not properly regarded as divine in their nature. It was also applied to a disembodied soul, which was conceived as the image of the body in which it once dwelt, as, for example, we read in First Samuel (ch. 38, v. 13), the witch of Endor saw "Elohim ascending out of the earth," meaning thereby some being or disembodied spirit of an unearthly, superhuman character.

This word "Elohim" was the plural form of "Eloah" and was also used to denote the gods of the heathen. It was a generic name given to supernatural characters of all kinds having quasicorporeal forms, as well as to the gods of different tribes. Chemosh, Dagon, Baal, Yahveh were all known as Elohim and each of them had a human form. But in spite of its plural meaning the Hebrew prophets used it especially for Yahveh the God of Israel. The Israelites, however, believed Yahveh to be immeasurably superior to the Elohim of other tribes; while the inscription on the

Moabite stone shows that King Mesa held Chemosh to be as unquestionably the superior of Yahveh. It is said: "So now Yahveh the Elohim of Israel hath dispossessed the Amorites from before His people Israel, and shouldst thou possess it? Wilt not thou possess that which Chemosh thy Elohim giveth thee to possess?" (Judges xi, 23, 24.) The Israelites of those days considered the difference between one Elohim and another to be one of degree and not of kind. The same word was likewise applied to Teraphim, the images of family gods which were only deceased ancestors. Laban asks his son-in-law most indignantly, "Wherefore hast thou stolen my Elohim?"

From a careful study of the Old Testament we see that, although the Israelites believed in many kinds of Elohim and used the word indiscriminately, Yahveh was the God of their tribe, while other tribes had Elohim of their own. When the house of Israel conquered any other tribe, their tribal

God Yahveh stood at the head of the gods of the conquered tribe, as we know from history. When the Babylonians and Chaldeans were conquered by the Israelites, Yahveh was placed above Bel, Baal, Merodoch, Moloch, and the other Elohim or gods of the conquered tribes. Thus by the gradual process of evolution Elohim or Yahveh became the king or Lord of all gods. We can now easily understand what the Hebrew Psalmist meant when he said: "Among the gods there is none like unto thee, the king above all gods." But although Yahveh became the supreme Lord of all gods, hence of all tribes and nations, he still did not lose his human form, human attributes and human personality. Even when he became the creator and ruler of the universe, he had the same human form, the same attributes and personality as were ascribed to him by the ancient Israelites. A belief in many gods was at the foundation of the Judaic conception of one Supreme Being, and Yahveh, the tribal god originally worshipped under the form of a bull, gradually evolved into "god of gods" and finally into the one and only God of the universe.

In like manner it can be shown that among the ancient Greeks and other Aryan nations the idea of a personal God with a human form gradually developed from a belief in many tribal gods or nature gods. All monotheistic conceptions can be traced back to polytheistic beliefs. The ancient Greeks, like all other primitive peoples, worshipped many nature gods. They perceived the forces of nature and gave to them human powers and attributes. We know that Zeus, Apollo, Athene were all personified powers of nature. Zeus originally meant sky, hence god of the sky, the god of rain or rainer. The old prayer of the Athenians was "Rain, rain, O dear Zeus, on the land of the Athenians and on the fields." Here "O dear Zeus" or dear sky at once brings in the personal element. "Dear sky" refers to the god of the sky, the governor of rain. Apollo again was the sun god; Athene, the dawn-goddess. Each of these mythological deities was, furthermore, originally the god of some family or clan, and afterward when one family became stronger than others, its family god stood at the head of the other gods; thus in course of time the ancient God Zeus-pitar or in Latin Jupiter, meaning in English Father in heaven, became the God of all gods and was supposed to be the God of all nations.

So it was in ancient India during the Vedic period. The Vedic poets at first personified the forces of nature and gave them human attributes and intelligence. They were called in Sanskrit "Devas" or "Bright Ones," such as Indra the rainer or thunderer, Agni the god of fire, Vâyu the god of storm or wind, Varuna the god of the sky, and so on. Eventually Varuna, lord of the sky, became Deva Deva, the God of all gods, and thus gradually arose in India the monotheistic conception of the Supreme personal God with human attributes. It can in the same way be shown that the tribal gods among the Semitic tribes were at first nothing but nature gods.

It may be asked here: Why were the forces of nature personified? Because primitive man could not help it. Wherever he saw any activity or motion, he compared it to the conscious activity of his own body or to the voluntary movements of his limbs, and explained this natural activity by imagining it to be the conscious act of some superhuman being, possessing will-power and intelligence, and who was called the mover. From this we can easily understand the reason for the ancient belief that all material objects like the sun, moon and stars, were moved by angels. Now we say "it rains" or "it thunders," but the primitive man used to say "he rains," "he thunders." In this manner the unscientific minds of ancient times came to a belief in natural agencies. These agents were like human beings, only more powerful than any mortal agent. Hence was developed the idea of superhuman beings who became tribal gods, who were invoked in time of need. The Lord of the universe and the king above all gods was necessarily infinitely more powerful than these superhuman agents of nature, but still he had a human form infinitely magnified in size, because it is extremely difficult for the human mind to go beyond the idea of a human God.

From ancient times, however, strong protests have been made by great thinkers against this human idea of God with human form and human attributes; but again and again these objections have been brushed aside by the vast majority of people. Xenophanes, the Greek philosopher, about the sixth century before Christ tried to overthrow this anthropomorphic conception of God. He said: "The Godhead is all eyes, all ears, all understanding, unmoved, undivided, calmly ruling everything by his thought, like men neither in form nor in understanding." The early Christians who were brought up in the schools of Plato and Aristotle also deprecated the idea of a human God. To them the Supreme Being was no longer simply Elohim or Yahveh, the Lord of the house of Israel; not merely the God of Abraham, Isaac and Jacob, the God who walked in the garden of Eden in the cool of the day and ate and drank; He was no longer even the God "who maketh the clouds His chariot, who walketh upon the wings of the wind," but a Supreme Being who was infinite, indescribable, unutterable, and whose form could not be seen with fleshly eyes, whose voice could not be heard with mortal ear, whose size was incomprehensible. Clement of Alexandria says: "There is no name that can properly be named of Him; neither the one, nor the good, nor mind, nor absolute being, nor Father, nor creator, nor Lord can be the appropriate name for Him." And Cardinal Newman declares: "God is incommunicable in all His attributes."

Not very long ago the Bishop of London also protested against the human God, saying: "There is a sense in which we cannot ascribe personality to the unknown, absolute Being; for our sense of personality is of necessity compassed with limitations, and from these limitations we find it impossible to separate our conception of a person." When, indeed, we speak of human personality, we include not only age, but sex, character, outward appearance, the expression of the face and so on.

Those who believe in a personal God with a human form and human attributes do not consider these limitations. They do not think for a moment: How is it possible for the infinite eternal Being to be confined within the limits of a human form, however magnified it may be? How is it possible for the Absolute Being to come under the limitations of time and space? Physical form is nothing but limitation in space and time and if the eternal and infinite God be above time and space, how can He have a physical form? Yet most of the dualistic religions teach that

God has a form, and ask us to believe in it and to worship Him as one with form. How are we going to reconcile this self-contradictory statement that God is the infinite, eternal Being with a finite form? We do not find any solution of the difficulty in any of the Scriptures of the three great Semitic religions—Judaism, Christianity and Mahometanism. Of these Christianity conceives God under a triune form, while Judaism and Mahometanism insist on the absolute unity of the Supreme Being. Where is then the solution of the problem? If God be infinite and all-pervading, how can He have form?

The dualists or monotheists believe in the Supreme Being with a human form, but they say that that form is not material or physical but spiritual. It cannot be seen by the physical eye, but it can be seen by the spiritual eye of an enlightened soul. According to the dualistic system of religion in India, the infinite, eternal, unknowable Being or substance of the universe, which is called in Sanskrit *Brahman*, is the source of all powers and all forms. Although it is formless like the infinite ocean of reality or of absolute existence, intelligence and bliss, it nevertheless contains in a potential state all the forms of the waves that can arise in that eternal ocean. The water of the ocean has no particular form or shape; we can say that it is formless in one sense, but at the same time it can take any form when frozen into ice. A block of ice, for instance, can appear in the form of a triangle, a sphere, a circle, an animal or a human being. The same water without losing its nature can appear in a solidified form; and as in this case we are justified in saying that water, although formless, contains in a potential state all imaginable forms within itself, so the water of the ocean of that absolute Reality possesses in a potential state all the physical, material, mental and spiritual forms that ever existed, or ever will exist in future.

The infinite, eternal Brahman does, indeed,

appear and manifest itself with a spiritual form, in order to satisfy the desire of the devotee or worshipper. Wherever there is intense longing to see God, wherever there is unflinching devotion and unselfish love with the whole heart and soul, there is the manifestation of the formless One to fulfil the desire of the devotee. It is then that the invisible Brahman, or the Supreme Being, or the Reality, manifests itself and becomes visible to the spiritual eye of the worshipper. Intense longing, unswerving devotion and whole-hearted love of the soul draw out from the infinite source any particular form which the devotee wishes to see and worship; they have the power, as it were, to condense and solidify the water of the ocean of Reality into the various forms. The spiritual form of the Divinity rises in the ocean of formless Brahman or of the absolute Godhead, floats there for some time, and after satisfying the desires of the true Bhakta or worshipper, merges into that ocean again.

These forms vary in accordance with the ideal of the worshipper. If a worshipper has a longing to see God in the form to which he is devoted, of Jehovah or of Christ for instance, he must draw that out of the infinite ocean. The Divinity will appear in that form to satisfy the desire of that devotee. If he be devoted to the form of Buddha, or Krishna, or Râmakrishna, or any other human or imaginary form, he will see such an one with his spiritual eye through intense longing and love. The personal God with a spiritual form is the objectification, projection, manifestation of the impersonal ocean of Divinity. The highest of all such manifestations is the Iswara of Vedanta. He is worshipped under various names as Vishnu, Jehovah, Shiva, Father in heaven, or Allah. As all-pervading heat is imperceptible but becomes perceptible through friction, so wherever there is the intense friction of devotion and love in the soul of the worshipper, there is the manifestation of that infinite Being either in human or superhuman form.

There have been many such instances where the absolute omnipresent Being manifested itself in various forms among all nations and in all countries.

In ancient times there lived a boy saint who was the son of a ruling monarch. His name was Prahlâda. His father was absolutely materialistic and atheistic in his belief, and could not bear the idea of a ruler greater and more powerful than himself. He believed in no other ruler of the world and through vanity and egotism thought that he was the lord of all. His son Prahlâda, however, was a born saint. From his childhood his heart and soul were filled with extreme faith, devotion and love for the almighty Ruler and Lord of the universe. He cared nothing for the world and found no pleasure in the luxuries and comforts of a princely life. They did not attract his mind. He always preferred to stay alone and had a tendency to renounce everything. So deeply absorbed was his mind in his Divine Ideal that he could not listen to other things, and it was impossible for him to obey the commands of his godless father. The king grew angry at his behavior, and one day, calling the prince to him, he asked him the reason of his disobedience. He inquired under whose instigation he was behaving in that way and acting rebelliously against him who was the lord of all. The boy saint replied: "The ruler of the universe, the lord of all nations, who is greater and more powerful than your majesty, has captured my heart and soul and has inspired me to behave in this way." At this reply the king, furious with rage and anger, was ready to punish his son by killing him instantly. Drawing his sword, he cried: "How dost thou dare to say that thou hast a lord more powerful or stronger than I? Where is thy lord? Show him to me!" The boy answered: "He is everywhere." The king demanded, "Is he in that pillar?" Prahlâda, praying to his Divine Ideal from the bottom of his heart and soul and with firm faith, rejoined: "Yes, He is there in that pillar." The king answered: "Now ask thy lord to save thee from being beheaded." Thus saying, he struck the pillar with a giant's might and knocked it down. In the midst of the thundering noise of the crash appeared the divine figure, radiant with celestial glory, to protect the devotee of the Almighty Lord. The eyes of the wicked monarch were dazzled by the extraordinary brightness and celestial lustre of the divine form, but he could not bear the sight of another lord beside himself. He attacked the Divine manifestation and in his attempt to conquer the Supreme Ruler he fell breathless on the spot. Such was the power of true faith. Can any one question the power of true faith when Jesus said: "for verily I say unto you, if ye have faith as a grain of mustard seed, ye shall say unto this mountain 'remove hence from yonder place,' it shall remove; and nothing shall be impossible to you." (Matt. xvii, 20.) That faith brought out the manifestation of the omnipresent Lord from the pillar. At the sight of this wonderful Divine power and glory of the Almighty the soul of the boy saint was filled with unbounded joy and ecstatic happiness. He approached the mighty figure with awe, reverence and devotion, and prostrating himself at His feet, he poured forth all prayers before Him to his heart's content, saying: "O Lord, the Almighty Ruler of the universe, Thou art indeed all-pervading and almighty. Thy power is inscrutable. To save Thy child from imminent death, to fulfil the desire of Thy true devotee and to punish this vain and egotistical earthly monarch, Thou hast shown Thy power and glory to all by making this Thy superhuman manifestation. What words are adequate to describe Thy majesty and Thy loving-kindness? All words that we can utter are Thine! I am Thy child and Thy servant; keep me in Thy service forever and ever, O Lord and Father of all animate and inanimate beings of the universe."

"O Lord, Thou art the goal of all religions,

and the sustainer, the master, the witness, the habitation, the refuge and the friend of all living creatures; Thou art the origin, dissolution, support, end and the inexhaustible seed of the whole manifested universe. Thou art one, yet Thou takest many forms through Thy unspeakable power of Mâya. I bow down and salute Thee. Whosoever knows Thee as formless and with form knows the eternal Truth."

Fatherhood and Motherhood of God.

"*I am the Father and Mother of the universe.*"—Bhagavad Gita, ix, 17.

"*Why does the God-lover find such pleasure in addressing the Deity as Mother? Because the child is more free with its Mother, and consequently she is dearer to the child than any one else.*"—Life and Sayings of Râmakrishna, by F. Max Müller, p. 118.

Fatherhood and Motherhood of God.

THE religious history of the world shows that the conception of God as the Father of the universe first arose among the Aryan nations, and not among any of the Semitic tribes. It was in ancient India that the Aryans first worshipped the Supreme Being by addressing Him as the Father in Heaven. The origin of the English word "father" can be traced back through Latin "Pater" and Greek "Pitar" to Sanskrit "Pitar" meaning father. The Christians, however, believe that before the advent of Jesus the Christ, the fatherhood of the Almighty Being was unknown to the world.

Not very long ago the famous Rt. Rev. Bishop Potter of New York said in one of his lectures: "Go to India, to Burma, to China, to Greece; or to Egypt or Rome and see if anywhere among them all you will find a religion with any other idea of man than that he is the mere creature of his governor, his Pharaoh, his Sultan, his Rajah, his proconsul, or by whatever name you choose to call it." He also said: "It was Christ who brought an entirely new conception of the relation of God to men." Such statements, however, are neither founded upon truth nor supported by any historical evidence. On the contrary, it is a well-known fact that in India, from prehistoric times, the Hindu religion has given to man a position much higher than the Christian conception of his relation to his Maker. The ancient Vedic sages were the first to declare before the world that the human soul is not only the child of God but that it is essentially divine and in its true nature is one with the Supreme Being.

According to the Hebrew religion the

relation of God to man was like that of an absolute monarch to his subject, or like that of a master to his slave; while the religious history of the ancient Aryan nations testifies that they had risen to a much higher conception of God than as a despotic Ruler long before the Christian era. The Christian missionaries and preachers have been trumpeting before the world for several centuries that no religion outside of Christianity has ever inculcated the idea of the Fatherhood of God and that it was Christ alone who brought it to men from his celestial abode. Moreover, they are especially eager to impress upon the minds of their co-religionists that the Hindus in particular had no conception of a Heavenly Father, that they never knew the fatherly relation of God to man. But those who have studied carefully the history of the growth of Christianity are familiar with the fact that the idea of the Fatherhood of God did not originate with Jesus the Christ as modern Christians believe, but existed in the religious atmosphere of northern Palestine from the second century B.C. as a result of the Hellenic influence upon Judaism of the worship of Jupiter. Jesus took up this grand Aryan idea of the Fatherhood of God and emphasized it in his teachings more strongly than any of his predecessors had done in Palestine.* It was Yahveh that Christ worshipped as his Heavenly Father, it was Yahveh to whom he prayed as the Father of the universe; consequently, those who follow Christ and his teachings, worship their God through the same relation as was established by their Master. The worship of God is impossible without having some kind of relation between the worshipper and the object of worship.

The relation between father and son is much higher than that between the creator and his creatures as it had existed in Judaism. The transition from the Judaic relation between God and man to that of father and son was therefore a great step toward the

* See p. 173: *Son of God.*

realization of the spiritual unity of the individual soul and the universal Spirit. It was no longer an external relation to power and strength, but had become a kind of kinship, of internal blood relation such as exists between an earthly father and his son. There is a tie of love that binds a son to his father, and such a tie brings the individual soul nearer to the Creator of the universe. As the earthly father of an individual is ordinarily considered to be his creator because of his begetting him and bringing him into existence out of an invisible germ, so when the undeveloped mind began to think of the creation of the universe, it imagined that the creator was one who brought the world into existence and produced it out of nothing. Gradually the conception of the creator evolved into that of the father of the universe.

All our conceptions of God begin with anthropomorphism, that is, with giving to God human attributes in a greatly magnified degree, and end in de-anthropomorphism, or making Him free from human attributes. At the first stage the human mind conceives of the creator as a great Being who dwells outside of the world which he creates, just as the father is separate from the son whom he begets. The Hebrew conception of Yahveh was purely anthropomorphic. Yahveh possessed all human attributes and, dwelling in a heaven outside of the universe, created the world out of nothing, fashioned it, and afterward became its governor. The same Yahveh, when addressed by Jesus the Christ as the Father in heaven, did not lose his Yahvehic nature; but was simply endowed with the fatherly aspect of Jupiter or the Greek Zeus-pitar. The sweet, loving and fatherly attributes of Jupiter were superadded to the stern, extra-cosmic Yahveh, the despotic ruler of the world.

The word Jupiter, or Zeus-pitar, has a long history behind it, with which ordinary readers are not familiar, but which is known to a few Vedic scholars. It meant "father in heaven" and is a transmuted form of the Sanskrit Dyus-Pitar or Dyaus-Pitar, which very often occurs in the Rig Veda, the oldest of the revealed Scriptures of the world. The term "Dyaus" or "Dyus" originally signified "shining space" or "heavens," but afterwards it was used for the self-effulgent Spirit dwelling in the heavens; and "Pitar" was the father and the protector. In the second book of the Rig Veda (ch. iii, ver. 20) we read, "*Dyaus mê pitâ janitâ nâbhi ratra.*" Here the word "Dyaus" is used, not in the sense of "shining heavens" as some of the Oriental scholars have imagined, but it refers to the Spiritual Source of all light as well as of heavens. "Pitâ," literally "father," here means "protector." The meaning of this verse therefore is "That shining or self-effulgent Spirit who dwells in the heavens, is my father and protector, my progenitor or producer, and in him lies the source of all things." This was the earliest conception of the fatherly aspect of the Supreme Being which we find in studying the Vedas. Again, in the tenth book of the Rig Veda, Prajâpati, the Lord of all creatures, is addressed as "Pitar," the Father and the Protector (ch. v, ver. 6, 7).

The one Supreme personal God was called in the Vedas "Prajâpati," the Lord and Father of all creatures. He is most beautifully described in the one hundred and twenty-first hymn of the tenth book of the Rig Veda. The conception of a personal God which we find in this hymn has not been surpassed by the idea of a personal God among any other nation during the last five thousand years. When an ancient Vedic Seer was asked "To whom shall we offer our prayers and sacrifices?" he replied:

1. "In the beginning there arose the Prajâpati, the first-born Lord of all that exists. He holds by his power the heavens and the earth. To Him we should offer our prayers and sacrifices."

2. "Prajâpati, the Lord of all creatures, who gives life and strength to all that exists,

from whose body emanate the individual souls like sparks from fire; who is the purifier of all souls; whose commands all creatures revere and obey; whose shadow is immortality and mortality; to Him we should offer our prayers and sacrifices."

3. "Who by His power and glory became the one King (without a second) of all men, of beasts, nay, of all animate and inanimate objects; to Him we should offer our prayers and sacrifices.

4. "Whose greatness is manifested in the snow-capped ranges of mountains and in the waters of the rivers and the oceans; whose arms are spread on all sides; to Him should we offer our prayers and sacrifices.

5. "Who made the sky strong and the earth firm, who established heavens in their places, nay, the highest heaven; who measured the light in the air; to Him we should offer our prayers and sacrifices.

6. "To whom heaven and earth, standing firm by His help, look up, trembling in their

minds, and by whose support the rising sun shines forth. To Him we should offer our prayers and sacrifices.

7. "When the great waters went everywhere, holding the germ and generating fire, thence He arose who is the sole life of the bright spirits (Devas). To Him we should offer our prayers and sacrifices.

8. "Who is the one Lord of all living beings and God above all gods; who by His might looked over the causal waters at the time of dissolution. To Him we should offer our prayers and sacrifices.

9. "May He not injure us, He who is the Creator of the earth, heavens, and bright and mighty waters, who is the foundation of truth, righteousness and justice. To Him we should offer our prayers and sacrifices.

10. "O Prajâpati, no other but Thou has held together all these phenomena; whatever we desire in sacrificing to Thee, may that be ours; may we be the lords of all wealth."

The same Prajâpati, the true, just and

righteous Lord of the universe and God of all gods, was addressed by the Vedic Sage as "Dyaus-Pitar" or the Father in heaven and the Protector of all. He is described in another hymn of the Rig Veda as *Aditi*, the unflinching and immutable support of the phenomenal universe. The word "Aditi" signified the motherly aspect of the Divine Being. "Aditi is in the heavens and in the illumined space that pervades between heaven and earth, the Mother of all Devas or gods as well as the Creator of all animate and inanimate objects. She is also the Father and Protector of all; She is the Son and the Creator; by Her grace She saves from sin the souls of those who worship Her. She gives unto Her children everything that is worth giving. She dwells in the forms of all Devas or bright spirits; She is all that is born and all that will be born. She is all in all." (Rig Veda, Book 2, ch. vi, verse 17.)

Thus we see that in ancient India God was conceived as both the Father and the

Mother of the universe centuries before Jesus was born. In Greece, however, the idea of the Fatherhood of Zeus-pitar prevailed, but his motherly aspect was denied, because Zeus-pitar or Jupiter was only an extra-cosmic personal God. As long as the conception of God is extra-cosmic, or as dwelling outside of nature, so long He appears to His worshippers as father alone and as masculine. The God of Jesus the Christ was the same extra-cosmic creator who was called Yahveh or Jehovah in Judaism and who was always described as masculine.

According to the Hebrews the masculine element of nature possessed all activity, strength and power; the male principle was recognized as the generator, and the female principle of nature was thought to be lower, insignificant, powerless and passive. The female principle of nature was the producer and bearer of what the male principle created; consequently everything that represented the female principle was considered as unimportant. This explains why womanhood was estimated so low by the writers of the Old and New Testaments, especially by the great apostle to the Gentiles. Even the very appearance and existence of woman on earth depended upon a man's rib, according to Genesis. Although the Creator was represented by the Hebrews as masculine and all-powerful, when they explained the genesis of the world they could not deny the presence of the feminine element which helped the Creator in bringing life into existence. In the Mosaic account of Genesis we read "And the spirit of God moved upon the face of the waters" (Gen. i, 2), which literally means that the Creator impregnated the waters or the female element of nature. And, as God, that is, the male element, was extra-cosmic, outside of nature, and possessed all activity and power, He became the object of worship; and the female element or nature was entirely ignored. Every Christian admits the existence of nature, the female principle; but she has never been worshipped or adored. The idea of Father grew stronger and stronger and the mother nature was left aside as passive and powerless, and was ultimately ignored. As long as the conception of God remains as extra-cosmic, separate from nature which is passive, so long will He appear as Father alone. The more we comprehend God as immanent and resident in nature, the more clearly we understand that God is our Mother as well as our Father. When we see that nature or the feminine principle is inseparable from the Supreme Being or the masculine element, when we realize that nature is not passive and powerless but the Divine Energy, then we understand that God is one stupendous Whole, in whom exist both the masculine and feminine principles. Then we no longer separate nature from God, but we recognize nature as a part of the manifested Divine Energy.

So long as God is supposed to dwell outside of nature and as father alone, He remains as the efficient cause of the universe, while nature appears to be the material cause. But when we realize that nature or the material cause is nothing but a part of the manifested Divine Energy, we then understand that God does not, like a carpenter or a potter, create or fashion the phenomena out of the materials which exist outside of Himself, but that He projects by the process of evolution everything out of His own body wherein dwell all matter and forces of the world.

In no other Scriptures than the Vedas, in no other religion than that of Vedanta, is the personal God described as the Father and the Mother, the efficient and the material cause of the universe. Now-a-days liberal-minded Christians are trying to introduce the idea that God is both Father and Mother of the universe; but they do not realize that by so doing they are entirely upsetting the Christian conception of God, who dwells outside of nature and of the universe. The God of Christianity can never become both Father and Mother at the same time. If we address Him as the Mother of the universe, we have outgrown that conception of God which is taught in the Bible and in Christian theology. In the whole Scriptures of the Christians there is not one passage where Jehovah is addressed as the Mother. In Isaiah (ch. lxvi, 13) the Lord says: "As one whom his mother comforteth so will I comfort you." From this passage, however, no fair-minded person can deduce that Jehovah was the mother of the universe.

The Vedantic idea that God is the Mother as well as the Father of all harmonizes with the modern scientific conception of God. Modern science traces the whole phenomenal universe back to the state of eternal energy. The doctrine of evolution, correlation of forces, persistence of energy, all these clearly prove that the phenomena of the whole universe and the various forces of the external and internal world are but the expressions of one eternal energy. The theory of evolution explains only the mode in which that eternal energy produces this phenomenal universe. Science has disproved the old theory of creation out of nothing through the fiat of an extra-cosmic God, and has shown that something can never come out of nothing. Science teaches that the universe existed in a potential state in that energy, and gradually through the process of evolution the whole potentiality has become kinetic or actual. That eternal energy is not an unintelligent energy, but is intelligent. Wherever we cast our eyes, either in the external or internal world, we find the expression, not of a fortuitous or accidental combination of matter and mechanical forces, but of regular laws guided by definite purpose. This universe is not a chaos but a cosmos, one harmonious whole. It is not an aimless chain of changes which we call evolution, but there is an orderly hidden purpose at every step of evolution. Therefore, that energy is intelligent. We may call this self-existing, intelligent, eternal cosmic energy the Mother of the universe. She is the source of infinite forces and infinite phenomena. This eternal energy is called in Sanskrit *Prakriti* (Latin *procreatrix*), the creative power of the universe.

"Thou art the *Parâ Prakriti* or the divine energy of the Supreme Being. Of Thee is born everything of the universe, therefore Thou art the Mother of the universe." As all the forces of nature are but the manifestations of this Divine Energy, She is called all-powerful. Wherever there is the expression of any force or power in the universe, there is the manifestation of the eternal Prakriti or the Divine Mother. It is more appropriate to call that Energy mother than father, because like a mother, that Energy holds within her the germ of the phenomenal universe before evolution, develops and sustains it, projects it on space and preserves it when it is born. She is the Mother of the Trinity, Creator, Preserver and Destroyer. She is the source of all activity. She is the *Sakti*, force in action.

A creator, when deprived of his creative power, is no longer the creator. As the creative power is one of the expressions of that eternal Energy, the Creator or Brahma is looked upon by the Hindus as the child of the universal Divine Mother, so, too, is the Preserver Vishnu and the Destroyer Siva. The Hindus have understood this Eternal Energy as the Mother of the universe and have worshipped Her from the prehistoric times of the Vedic period. Here we should remember that this Divine Energy is not the same as the powerless and passive nature which was rejected and ignored by the Jews and the Christians. We must not mistake this worship of the Divine Mother for Nature-worship. In the Rig Veda we read: "The Mother Divine says, 'I am the Queen of the universe, the giver of all wealth and fruits of works. I am intelligent and omniscient. Although I am one, by My powers I appear as manifold. I cause war for protecting men, I kill the enemy and bring peace on earth.

I stretch out heaven and earth. I have produced the Father. As the wind blows by itself, so I produce all phenomena by My own will. I am independent and responsible to none. I am beyond the sky, beyond this earth. My glory is the phenomenal universe; such am I by My power.'"*

Thus the Divine Mother is described as all in all. We live and move and have our existence in that Divine Mother. Who can live for a moment if that Eternal Energy cease to manifest? All our mental and physical activity depends on Her. She is doing whatever She chooses to do. She is independent. She obeys none. She is the producer of every event that occurs in the universe. She makes one appear good, spiritual and divine, while it is She who makes another appear as wicked and sinful; since it is through Her power one performs virtuous deeds or commits sinful acts. But She is beyond good and evil, beyond virtue and vice. Her forces are

* Rig Veda, x, *hymn*, 125.

neither good nor evil, although they appear so to us when we look at them from different standpoints and compare them with one another.

When that all-pervading divine energy manifests, it expresses itself in two sets of opposite forces. The one set has the tendency towards God and is called *Vidyâ* in Sanskrit. The other tends towards worldliness and is called *Avidyâ*. The one leads to freedom and happiness, and the other to bondage and suffering. The one is knowledge, the other is ignorance. The one is light, the other is darkness. Each individual soul is a center where these opposite forces are constantly working and fighting with one another. When *Vidyâ* or the powers which lead Godward predominate, we advance towards God and become religious, spiritual and unselfish; but when its opposite, the *Avidyâ* power prevails, we become worldly, selfish and wicked. When the former is predominant the latter is overcome, and *vice versa*. These powers exist in each individual, though they vary in the degree of intensity in each. The man or woman, in whom the former, that is, the Godward-leading-powers prevail, is called devotional, prayerful, righteous, pure in heart, unselfish. These qualities are but expressions of the *Vidyâ* powers within us. Such higher powers are latent in all, even in those who do not show virtuous qualities. All persons can rouse those latent spiritual forces by practising devotion, prayer, righteousness, purity, unselfishness. The easiest way to attain them is by the worship of the *Vidyâ Sakti*, or that aspect of the Divine Mother or Divine Energy which represents all the powers that lead to spiritual perfection.

By worship or devotion is meant constant remembrance of that aspect. If we constantly think of the source of all spirituality and of all the higher powers which make one spiritual, surely those powers will be aroused in us, and we shall become spiritual, righteous and unselfish. Therefore the

Hindus worship this *Vidyâ Sakti.* When they worship that aspect, they do not, however, deny, or ignore its opposite nature which leads to worldliness, but they make it subordinate to the higher *Vidyâ* aspect. Sometimes they think of these opposite forces separately, personify them and make them the female attendants of the Divine Mother. The Divine Mother has many attendants. All the evil forces of nature are Her attendants. She stands in the center of the universe radiant in Her own glory, like the sun when surrounded on all sides by thick, dark clouds.

Wherever there is any expression of extraordinary righteousness and spirituality, it is a special manifestation of the Divine Mother, there is Her incarnation. The Divine Mother incarnates sometimes in the form of a man, and sometimes in the form of a woman, to establish order and righteousness. All men and women are Her children. But there is something more in woman. As woman represents motherhood on earth, so all women, whether married or unmarried, are representatives of that Almighty Divine Mother of the universe. It is for this reason that women are so highly revered and honored by the Hindus. There is no country in the world except India where God the Supreme Being has been worshipped from time immemorial as the Divine Mother of the universe. India is the only country where the earthly mother is looked upon as the living Deity, and where a man learns in his childhood "One mother is greater than a thousand fathers."

You have heard many stories regarding the condition of women in India. Most of these, however, are grossly exaggerated, some are utterly false and some are partially true. The familiar American story of Hindu mothers throwing their babes into the Ganges to become food for crocodiles, is unknown among the Hindus. In the first place, crocodiles cannot live in a strong current like that of the Ganges. I have travelled the length of this mighty river from its mouth to its source, some fifteen hundred miles, but never found a single instance of such an inhuman act. Hindu mothers, like their Christian sisters, may sometimes destroy their children, but such action is as strongly condemned in India as in America. These statements were heard by me for the first time after coming to America, though tales and pictures to this effect have been quite common in this country in books for the young.* There is no other country "Where every living mother"—as Sir Monier Monier Williams says—"is venerated as a kind of deity by her children, where every village or city has its special guardian mother, called (in Sanskrit) *Mata.*" *

It is extremely difficult for a Western mind to grasp exactly what the Hindus mean when they say that every woman is a representative of the Divine Mother. A very simple illustration will give you an idea of the respect the Hindus have for women. In Sanskrit when two names are used together, the rule of

* "Hinduism and Brahmanism," p. 222.

grammar is that the more honorable should stand first. In Sanskrit we say women and men, not men and women; instead of father and mother, we say mother and father; instead of husband and wife, wife and husband, because a woman is always more honorable than a man. In India wives do not adopt their husbands' names, they do not merge their individuality into that of their husbands as women do in the West, but they keep their own name separate. If a wife's name be Râdhâ, and her husband's name be Krishna, and if we say them together, we would say Râdhâ-Krishna and never Krishna-Râdhâ. The wife's name must be said first. So we say Sitâ-Râma; Sitâ is the wife and Râma is the husband. Again, when God incarnates in a man form, as in Krishna or Râma, the wife of such an incarnation will be worshipped as the incarnation of the Mother. The wife will be worshipped first and then the husband. A Western mind does not easily appreciate the wonderful reverence for womanhood which the Hindus have.

The Divine Mother is the personal God, the same as Iswara in Sanskrit; and Brahman or the Absolute Substance or the Universal Spirit is the impersonal Being. Brahman is formless, nameless and without any attributes. It is the ocean of absolute intelligence, existence and bliss. It has no activity. It is the Godhead of Fichte, the Substantia of Spinoza. It transcends all phenomena. Before phenomenal manifestation Divine Energy rested on the bosom of that ocean of Absolute Being in a potential state. It is the dormant state of activity somewhat like our deep sleep state when all activity is latent. As in deep sleep all the mental and physical powers exist in us in an unmanifested condition and nothing is lost, so, before the beginning of the cosmic evolution, all the phenomenal forces of the universe remained dormant in that Energy. There were no phenomena, no manifestation of any powers whatever.

Again, as in our waking state all the latent powers manifest and we are able to walk, move, talk and are tremendously active, so, when a portion of that Impersonal Being wakes up, as it were, and manifests the latent cosmic powers of the sleeping Energy, the evolution of the cosmic Energy begins and the Impersonal Being appears as the Creator of the universe and its Preserver.

The Impersonal Being is then called personal, on account of that manifested energy. According to the Hindus the impersonal Brahman is neither masculine nor feminine. But the personal God is masculine and feminine both in one. Energy and Being are inseparable in the personal God. As pure Being without energy cannot produce any phenomena and as Energy possesses all activity and is the mother of all forces and phenomena, the personal God is most appropriately called the Mother of the universe. As fire and its burning power or heat are inseparable, so Being and Energy are inseparable and one.

Those who worship the masculine aspect of God, in reality worship the male child born of that Divine Mother. Because the activity, strength and power which make one masculine, owe their origin to that Divine Energy. But those who worship the Divine Mother worship the Whole—all gods, all angels and all spirits that exist in the universe.

The wonderful effect of this conception of the Motherhood of God is to be found in the daily life of almost every Hindu woman and man. A Hindu woman thinks that she is a part of the Divine Mother, nay one with Her. She looks upon all men and women of the world as her own children. She thinks of herself as the blessed Mother of the world. How can such a woman be unkind to anybody? Her pure motherly love flows towards all men and women equally. There is no room for any impure thought or feeling or passion in such a heart. That perfect motherly feeling makes her ultimately live like the Divine Mother on earth. Her ideal God in human form is her own child. She worships the incarnation of God as her most beloved child. Just as Mary was the Mother of Jesus, so the Hindu women in India often look upon themselves as the mother of Krishna, the Hindu Christ, or of Râma, another incarnation. Christian mothers, perhaps, will be able to appreciate this to a certain extent. If a Christian mother thinks that she is Christ's mother and loves Him as she loves her own child, the effect will be wonderful. She will then understand what Divine Motherhood is. The Hindus think this the easiest way for women to attain to that love which makes them unselfish and divine. A mother can sacrifice everything for her child; she naturally loves the child without seeking any return, though there are mothers who do not possess pure, unselfish motherly love. A true mother, however, loves her child above everything. If such a child be an incarnation of God Himself, how easy it will be for the mother to attain to the highest goal of religion. I know a lady in India who became a widow when she was young. She did not marry again. She was not like the ordinary woman of the world who thinks that a husband is essential to her happiness and that marriage is the highest ideal of life. She lived the pure life of a nun and worshipped Krishna as her own child. She became so advanced in spirituality that now hundreds of educated men and women of high rank in Calcutta come to see her, to receive spiritual instruction from her. They kiss the dust of her feet as devout Roman Catholics kiss the feet of the statue of Mary, they revere her and call her the Mother of God, Mother of Krishna, the Shepherd. She is still living near Calcutta. She feels in herself the presence of the blessed Mother of the universe.

Another wonderful result of this conception of God as the Mother of the universe, is that when a man worships God as his mother, he always thinks of himself as a child in its Mother's arms. As a child does not fear anything when it is near its mother, so the worshipper of the Divine Mother is never afraid of anything. He sees the Blessed Mother everywhere. In every woman he sees the manifestation of his Eternal Mother. Consequently, every woman on earth is his mother. He conquers all lust and sense desires. He sees woman in a different light. He worships every woman mentally.

I have seen a man who lived on this earth like a living child of the Divine Mother, always protected and taken care of by Her. He worshipped God as the Mother of the universe. Through that worship he became pure, righteous and spiritual. He used to say "O, my Mother, Thou art all in all. Thou art my Guide, my Leader and Strength." His Divine Mother showed him the true nature of man and woman. He bowed down before all women, young, mature and old, and said to them—"You are the living representatives of my Divine Mother on earth." How can a child have any other relation to one who is the same as its real mother? By this kind of devotion he conquered all lust and worldliness. His child-like, whole-souled and rapturous self-consecration to the Divine Mother is a landmark in the religious history of India. His whole life, which was the personification of purity, self-control, self-resignation and filial love to the Divine Mother, stands as a mighty testimony to the reality and effectiveness of the worship of God as the Mother of the universe. When he sang the praises of the Divine Mother, he gave life to every word he uttered, and no soul could hear him without being moved to tears by deep devotional feelings, without realizing that this wonderful child was in direct communion with his Divine Mother. His Divine Mother showed him that each woman was Her incarnation, so he worshipped and honored all women as a son might worship his own mother. Some Western people may laugh at such reverence, but a Hindu is extremely proud of it. He knows how to honor a woman. Professor Max Müller was much impressed with the wonderful life of this great sage, and recently published his life and sayings.* He was once asked: "If we are the children of your Divine Mother, why does She not take care of us? Why does She not come to us and take us up in Her arms?" The sage replied: "A mother has several children. To one she has given a doll, to another some candy, to the third a music box, according as each one likes. Thus when they begin to play and are absorbed, they forget their mother; she in the meanwhile looks after her household work. But the moment any one of them gets tired of the play, and, throwing aside the plaything, cries for the mother, 'Mamma, mamma dear!' she runs quickly to him, takes him up in her arms, kisses him often and often and caresses him. So, oh man! being absorbed with the playthings of the world you have forgotten your Divine Mother; when you get tired of your play, and, throwing aside the toys, you cry

* "Life and Sayings of Râmakrishna," by F. Max Müller. Charles Scribner's Sons, New York.

for Her sincerely and with the simplicity of a child, She will come at once and take you up in Her arms. Now you want to play and She has given you all that you need at present." Each one of us will see the Divine Mother sooner or later. The Mother is always taking care of us and protecting us whether we feel it or not, whether we realize it or not.

The Vedanta philosophy recognizes both the fatherhood and motherhood of the personal God and teaches us that through the worship of either of these aspects the highest ideal of religion can be reached. The Prajâpati or the Lord of all creatures of the Vedas is called "Iswara" in Vedanta. Some worship Him as the Father, while others call Him Divine Mother. But He is sexless and therefore both Father and Mother of all. Those who address Him as the Father say:

"O Lord, Thou art the Father of the universe, of all animate and inanimate objects. Thou art worshipped by all. Thou art greater than the greatest; O Thou of incomparable power, none in the heavens and earth is equal to Thee, how can any one be greater? O Lord, as a father forgiveth his son, a friend his dear friend, a lover his beloved, even so do Thou forgive me."

Those who worship His motherly aspect pray to Her, saying:

"O Mother Divine, Thou art the eternal energy, the infinite source of the universe. Thy powers manifest in the infinite variety of names and forms. Being deluded by the power of ignorance we forget Thee and take pleasure in the playthings of the world. But when we come to Thee, take Thy refuge and worship Thee, Thou makest us free from ignorance and worldliness, and givest us eternal happiness by keeping us, Thine own children, on Thy bosom."

The Relation of Soul to God.

"The soul enchained is 'man,' and free from chain is 'God.'"—Life and Sayings of Râmakrishna, by F. Max Müller, p. 145.

The Relation of Soul to God.

A CLEAR understanding of man's relation to God is a matter of momentous importance to students of philosophy and religion and to all seekers of Truth. From very ancient times all the best thinkers, prophets and the great religious leaders of the world, whether of the East or of the West, have endeavored to explain our relation to God and to the universe. Out of those explanations have arisen various schools of philosophy and different systems of religious beliefs among the different nations of the world.

Every philosophy and every religion, ancient or modern, has arrived at certain conclusions in its attempt to describe the relation which each individual bears to God. All such conclusions, of course, presuppose the existence of God, and depend upon the nature of our conception of God as well as of the human soul. Those who deny the existence of God and hold that we are but mere accidental appearances in the mechanical process of the blind forces of nature which are acting aimlessly upon dead matter, think that it is loss of time and waste of energy to discuss such useless and absurd topics. They would rather devote their energy to obtaining the best things of the Godless world for the comforts of the soulless body. They do not believe in the existence of any such thing as soul, mind or spirit apart from the functions of the body. When the body dies everything comes to an end. As with the body, so it is with the material universe.

Such thinkers are not the products of the Twentieth Century alone, but they are as old as the appearance of man upon earth. In ancient India this class of thinkers existed side by side with the believers in the individual soul of man and in God, as numerously as we find them to-day among the most cultivated minds of the West. Those ancient materialists, like the modern agnostics and atheists, making sense perception the standard of their knowledge of things, denied the existence of that which they could not perceive by their senses. But the other class of thinkers, who went below the surface of sense perceptions into the realm of the invisible, weighed these materialistic arguments, pointed out their fallacies, and ultimately established through logical and scientific reasoning, the existence of the individual soul of man as well as of the soul of the universe, or God, and described their mutual relation.

These thinkers can be divided into three classes: First, the dualists; secondly, the qualified non-dualists, and thirdly, the non-dualists, or monists. The Western dualists believe in an extra-cosmic personal God, who creates the universe out of nothing, fashions it, gives names to the phenomena, and afterwards governs it. According to them, God, the creator and governor of the universe, is eternally separate from the world and from all living creatures, just as a potter is separate from the pot which he makes or as a carpenter who stands always outside of the table or chair which he makes. The dualists believe in a God who has human attributes infinitely magnified. He is all-wise, merciful, just and all-powerful. Some of the dualists go so far as to give human form to God, as we find in the conception of Jehovah among the Hebrews and the orthodox Christians. In the Old Testament, Jehovah is described as walking with Adam in the Garden of Eden. It is said: "And they heard the voice of the Lord God walking in the garden in the cool of the day, and Adam and his wife hid themselves from the presence of the Lord God amongst the trees of the garden." (Genesis iii, 8.) Moses and Aaron, Nadab and Abihu, and seventy of the elders of Israel saw Him. The nobles not only saw but they did eat and drink with Him. (Exodus xxiv, 9, 11.) Moses saw Jehovah's back. Jehovah ate with Abraham under the oaks at Mamre. (Genesis xviii, 1, 8.) God was pleased with the sweet savor of Noah's sacrifice. He possessed human appetites. He walked with Noah.

The same Jehovah with a human form and human qualities and with a human personality is the ideal God of the orthodox Christian monotheists of to-day. They believe in Jehovah as sitting on a throne somewhere in the heavens, with eyes red with anger and revenge, and holding a rod, ever ready to punish the wicked with eternal fire. From many of the orthodox pulpits the same God is preached to-day, as He was in the days of the past. The relation of man to such a personal, or rather human God, with human attributes, is like that of a creature to his creator, of a subject to his king, or of a slave to his master. As the duty of a subject is to obey implicitly the commands of his king, or ruler, or governor, so every man's duty is to obey the commands of the Governor of the universe, otherwise he will be punished. Similar relation of man to the extra-cosmic personal Ruler of the universe is to be found in most of the dualistic or monotheistic religions of the world. All the religions of Europe and Asia which are dualistic or monotheistic teach that our relation to God is that of a creature to his creator, or of the governed to the governor.

Although man is said to be created in God's image in Genesis, yet it is generally understood that he cannot have any relation higher than that of a creature to his creator. It simply means that the first man, being the image of God, possessed at first some of the divine qualities before he was tempted by Satan. Although the Christians believe that Jesus the Christ was the son of God, and that God is the father of the universe, yet according to them, an ordinary mortal cannot be called the son of God in the same sense as Jesus of Nazareth was, because he was an exception to the general rule. Whether

Jesus ever meant that he was the only begotten son of God exclusive of any other mortal, is a problem yet to be solved. If every individual be a true image or the son of God, then the question arises, why should He punish His own son so mercilessly with eternal fire as is described in the parable of the marriage of the king's son: "Then said the king to the servants, bind him hand and foot and take him away and cast him into outer darkness; there shall be weeping and gnashing of teeth; for many are called but few are chosen." (Matt. xxii, 13, 14.) Again, in the saying: "Ye serpents, ye generation of vipers, how can ye escape the damnation of hell?" (Matt. xxiii, 33.) Thus, according to popular Christianity, as it is understood and preached in the orthodox churches, man's relation to God is not like that of His image, nor like that of a son to his loving Father, but like that of a subject to his despotic monarch, Christ being the only begotten son of God. The Christians believe that God creates the soul out of nothing and implants it in the human form at the time of its birth. As long as there is preached the idea of the creation of the universe and of man out of nothing by an extra-cosmic personal God with human attributes, so long will our relation to God remain like that of a creature to his creator or of the governed to his governor.

In India too there are dualists. They believe in an extra-mundane personal God who is the repository of all blessed qualities, who is omnipotent, omniscient, and all-loving; who creates the universe, not out of nothing, but out of the material of nature, which is eternal. God is the efficient cause of the universe and nature is the material cause. They do not believe that the human soul comes into existence all of a sudden and has a beginning, as the Christians do, but that it existed in the past and will exist in future from eternity to eternity. They say that as nature is eternal so are the individual souls. Each soul after remaining potentially in nature for some time, comes out of the causal state at the beginning of a new cycle of creation or evolution, and manifests in gross forms, one after another, going through the different grades of evolution according to its desires and tendencies, until it reaches perfection. After reading the New Testament one cannot get any definite conception of the nature of the human soul, nor of its destiny, but in the dualistic system of India one learns that the human soul is like an infinitesimal particle of nature containing the divine light of intelligence and divine power in an infinitely small degree, whose duty is to serve God through prayers, good deeds, good thoughts and love. God loves all, and He can be loved in return. Those who worship Him through unswerving devotion and unselfish love obtain freedom from the dark side of nature; that is, from the bondages of ignorance, selfishness, suffering, misery and all other imperfections; and after death they live a life of bliss and perfection forever in the presence of the eternal personal

God. This is salvation according to the dualists in India. They do not mean by salvation going to heaven, but on the contrary, hold that heaven is a realm where one goes to enjoy the results of one's good deeds, and at the end of such a period of celestial enjoyment one comes back to earth and is born again.

Each soul is bound to attain this salvation, sooner or later. Those who do wicked deeds reap the results of their actions and thoughts, not by going to any place of eternal fire and punishment, but by being born again and again until they reach the state of spirituality, devotion and righteousness. The monotheists in India do not believe that God punishes any one, as He is the embodiment of Divine love. Nor do they believe in eternal suffering, nor in any Satan or creator of evil. But they do believe in a temporary suffering of the wicked, which is the reaction of their own wicked acts. They do not blame God or charge Him with partiality, they do not blame Satan, but they take upon their own shoulders the whole burden of responsibility. These dualists believe that wherever there is life there is the manifestation of the divine light of intelligence, however small it may be, however imperfect the expression of intelligence may be. From the minutest insect up to the highest gods (Devas) or angels, or bright spirits, each individual life is filled with a ray of that Divine Sun. They sometimes compare God with a gigantic magnet and the individual soul with the point of a needle, and say as a magnet attracts a needle so the great God attracts the individual souls toward Him through love, and magnetizes them as it were by His divine grace and power. Although they believe that each soul is separate from God and from other souls, yet its relation to God is like that of a ray to the sun or of a spark to fire. Their conception of the human soul is with attributes, with qualities and character, with mind, intellect, sense-powers, and the finer particles of ethereal matter which give foundation to grosser physical forms. In short, it is the same as the individual ego, as we call it, or the spiritual body as it is called in the New Testament. According to these dualists, God can be worshipped by man through various relations, such as by calling Him master, or father, or mother, or brother, or friend, or son, or husband. These relations depend upon the nature and characteristics of the worshipper. Some like to think of themselves as servants of God, others as friends, or brothers, or sons. They say, as the same man in a household can be the master in relation to his servants, the father in relation to his children, a friend, a brother, or a husband in relation to his wife, so the same God can appear in all those various relations to different devotees according to their modes of thinking. Such is the conception of the individual soul and its relation to God according to the dualistic thinkers of India.

Next to the dualistic conception of God comes that of the qualified non-dualists.

These thinkers go a little deeper than the dualists. Starting from the dualistic standpoint they go a step further toward the realization of Truth and of man's relation to God. According to them, God is no longer extracosmic, no more outside of and separate from the universe, but He is intra-cosmic. He is no longer governor from the outside, but *Antaryâmin,* inter-ruler. He is immanent and resident in nature. He interpenetrates every particle of the universe. The physical universe is His gross physical body. He has infinite eyes, infinite ears, and infinite organs of other senses. He sees through the eyes of all living creatures of the universe. He hears through all the ears that exist in the universe. He has infinite heads. The wind is His breath. His mind is the sum total of individual minds, or in other words, the Cosmic Mind. His intellect is the Cosmic intellect. His soul is the Cosmic Ego, or the soul of the universe. He is no longer the creator of the universe, or one who fashions the materials of nature and gives names and forms to the phenomena from outside like a potter or a carpenter. He is not the efficient cause alone, as the dualists maintain, but He is both efficient and material cause of the universe. He creates, that is, He projects into the physical space the phenomenal forms out of nature or divine energy which is in His body. He is the one living Being in the universe. He is the one stupendous Whole, and we are but parts.

In that process of projection or evolution of nature, infinite numbers of individual souls which existed in His body from the beginningless past, come out on the physical plane, take forms, play their parts according to their desires, and fulfil the purpose of life by going through the process of evolution. Each individual soul is like a spark which emanates from the huge bonfire of God, and lives in and through God, but it cannot be called God. God dwells everywhere. He pervades the universe and nature, and yet He transcends them both. He is infinite but personal, without any human form. The qualified non-dualists say that God cannot be confined to any form, because every form is a limitation in space by time, while God is unlimited by space or time. He is beyond space and time. Still, He can appear in various forms to satisfy the desires of His worshippers. Our body is a part of God's body, our mind is a part of the divine or universal mind, our will is a part of the universal or cosmic will. This is called the qualified non-dualistic conception of God, because it looks at unity as qualified by variety. That is, God is one, the universe and human souls are one in God, yet each retains its own separate individuality. God is like a tree and we are like branches thereof. It reminds me of the simile of the vine and its branches which Jesus the Christ gave to show man's relation to God. The same idea underlies His saying, "My Father is greater than I." According to this class of thinkers the individual soul possesses all the qualities of the human ego. As our ego has mind, intellect, sense-power, memory, and is limited by other egos, so is the soul. After the death of the body the soul contracts its qualities within itself, and at the time of its birth it expands those latent powers. Our ego or soul is a part of the cosmic ego, or the soul of the universe, or God.

Next to these comes the class of monistic or non-dualistic thinkers. They do not stop where the qualified non-dualists have stopped, but they push their investigations still further, and analyze the nature of the individual soul or ego, and ultimately discover the unchangeable essence of the ego. They are the seekers of the unchangeable reality of the universe. In their search they will not stop until they have reached that Truth which is immutable, eternal and one. They adopt the scientific methods of analysis, observation and experiment, and apply them to solve the subtlest and most abstract problems. Analyzing the nature of the ego, they find that it cannot be the unchangeable reality or immutable Truth, because the mind, with its various modifications, such as intellect, memory, etc., is constantly changing. After patient research and continuous struggle to know the ultimate Truth, these great monistic sages realized that the ego, or the individual soul, is nothing but a changeful receptacle of a still subtler substance, which is unchangeable and eternal. They called it the Atman in Sanskrit.

There is no word in the English language which conveys the meaning of this Atman. It is much finer than ego or the living soul of the individual. Atman is the unconditioned reality in man; and the living soul or the individual ego is the subtle covering of the Atman, like the globe that covers the light of a lamp. That Atman is not a part of the universal ego, but it is one with the unconditioned Reality of the universe, which is called in Sanskrit Brahman, or the All-pervading Spirit, or the Absolute. Sometimes it is called Paramâtman, which was translated by Ralph Waldo Emerson as Over-Soul. It is finer than the Cosmic Ego or God. It is sexless, neither masculine nor feminine. It is sometimes translated by the Oriental scholars as the SELF. But Self is a confusing word. Some people mistake it for the Anglo-Saxon self, which acts and progresses, and which is another name for the ego.

According to the non-dualistic conception of the true nature of man, the Atman or the Self, or the spiritual essence of man, is the same as the Brahman, the spiritual or divine essence of the universe. The relation of the true nature of man to God is no longer like that of a creature to the Creator, nor like that of a son to his father, nor like that of a part to the whole, but it is absolute oneness on the highest spiritual plane. The Atman, or the divine nature of man, is the same as the absolute divinity of the Cosmos. On that highest spiritual plane there is no distinction, no idea of separation, no idea of creation. All ideas of separateness, all differentiations of phenomenal names and forms, merge into the absolute ocean of reality which is unchangeable, eternal and one. The essence of the Creator is infinite, and it interpenetrates the phenomenal forms as the external space pervades every particle of atoms of the phenomenal world. That essence is like the all-pervading background of the phenomenal appearances. Phenomena are like the waves in the ocean of Infinite Reality. Individual souls are like so many bubbles in that ocean of Absolute Existence. As a bubble rises on the surface of the ocean, takes a form, lives there, comes near other bubbles, lives in a group for some time, moves in the company of others, changes its size, perhaps, and goes down again; so the individual soul rises in that ocean of infinite existence, appears in various forms, passes through the different stages of evolution, and lives there for ever and ever, sometimes as manifested and at other times as unmanifested. The light of intelligence in the soul or ego is due to the reflection of the Atman or Divine Spirit on the mirror of the heart of the ego or soul. Therefore the soul is called the image or reflection of the Atman or Divine Spirit.

This idea is beautifully expressed in one of the Upanishads: "In the cave of our heart have entered the two—the Atman or the Divine Spirit, and the individual ego or soul. Dwelling on the highest summit, or the ether of the heart, the one witnesses the other, while the soul drinks the rewards of its own works. The wise men and sages describe the one as the light, and the other as the reflection, image or shadow." (Katha Upanishad, ch. iii, verse 1.) You will notice here what a deep meaning lies at the back of the expression, "Man is the image of God." The ancient Vedic sages used the same expression in a sense which many of the best philosophers of the Western world have failed to grasp or comprehend. Thus the most ancient Monistic sages explained the highest relation of the individual soul to Atman or Divine Spirit, by calling it the reflection or image of the Self-effulgent Light of God. But as a reflection cannot exist independent of the light whose reflection it is, so the soul of man cannot exist independent of Atman. Therefore the true nature of the soul is Atman, the divine and real spirit which cannot be divided into parts and is One Absolute Source of existence, intelligence and bliss. Such is the monistic or non-dualistic explanation of the relation of the soul to God.

Vedanta philōsophy recognizes these three explanations. It says that the relation of the soul to God varies as the conception of the individual soul and of God becomes finer and higher. Starting from the gross form of body, when a real and earnest seeker after Truth marches onward toward the Absolute, he passes through all the intermediate stages until he reaches that state of divine communion where he realizes the oneness of the Atman, or the true nature of man with Brahman, the cosmic Divine essence, or the Absolute Reality of the universe. Then he declares, I am Brahman, I am He, I am in the sun, in the moon, in stars; I am one with the All-pervading Reality; or as Jesus the Christ said, "I and my Father are one." He does not use the word "I" in its ordinary sense of ego or human personality, but in the sense of Atman, or Divine essence. Jesus was a dualist when He prayed to His Father in heaven, and he was a monist when He said, "I and my Father are one," "The kingdom of heaven is within you." A Vedanta philosopher or sage after realizing that absolute oneness on the highest spiritual plane of the Atman, says, when he returns to the plane of relativity and phenomena:

"O Lord, when I think of my body, I am Thy servant and Thou art my Master; when I look at my soul, I am Thy part and Thou art the one stupendous Whole; but when I realize my true nature, I am divine and one with Thee, the Absolute Spirit. Such is my conception of my relation to Thee."

What is an Incarnation of God?

"*The Lord says: 'Whenever religion declines and irreligion prevails I manifest myself to protect the righteous, to destroy evil and to establish true religion.'*"—Bhagavad Gita iv, 7, 8.

What is an Incarnation of God?

Two great religions of the world advocate the belief that God, the supreme Ruler of the universe, incarnates in human form to help mankind—the one is Christianity, the other is the religion of Vedanta which prevails in India.

Christianity, believing in the existence of one personal God who is the creator, governor and Father of the universe, teaches that this heavenly Father incarnated Himself in human form as Jesus the Christ to show His love, His mercy and kindness for His suffering children as well as to save the world from eternal perdition. It may be interesting to many to know how this doctrine of divine incarnation, unknown to the earliest Christians of the first century after Christ, gradually grew and developed into its present form. Readers of ecclesiastical history are well aware of the fact that no problem troubled the minds of the founders of the Christian church and of Christian theology so much as this one of the divine incarnation of Jesus the Christ. During the early periods of church history, indeed, no other question was considered to be of such vital importance as that of the heavenly Father's incarnation in the form of Jesus of Nazareth. Although for many of the uneducated masses this problem appears to have been satisfactorily solved by the wonderfully subtle and apparently logical arguments of certain priests and theologians, still it is not unknown to the educated classes that the acceptance of their solution depended largely upon priestly power, upon anathema and upon the persecution of those who refused to receive these arguments as the only correct solution of the problem.

Let us go back for a moment to that time when Constantine the Great settled the disputes of the bishops regarding the incarnation of the Supreme Being in the form of the Son of Man. In the first place we should remember that the modern Christian idea of divine incarnation is founded upon the belief in the Trinitarian doctrine of the Father, Son, and Holy Ghost in the memorable text of the First Epistle of John: "For there are three that bear record in heaven, the Father, the Word, and the Holy Ghost, and these three are one" (ch. v. 7). Before the doctrine of the divine incarnation of Jesus the Christ was established and accepted by the church, the early Christians believed in the Trinity and constantly discussed the most subtle and profound questions concerning the nature, generation, distinction and qualities of the three divine persons of the mysterious triad. At that time the majority of Christian thinkers believed in Jesus of Nazareth as the son of God, but they did not dare declare that he was "God himself in human form," the second principle of the blessed

Trinity. It was Justin Martyr, a Christian convert of the Platonic school and a believer in the Platonic doctrine of the Trinity, who about the middle of the second century for the first time promulgated the idea that Jesus the Christ, the son of God, was the second person in the Triune Deity and the creator of the universe. He is the earliest writer to whom the origin of this idea can be traced, and he did not ascribe his opinion to the Scriptures but to the special favor of God.

The Trinitarian controversies which first broke out in the Christian schools of Alexandria in Egypt, the land of Trinities, took a new form during the time of Constantine the Great, the chief point of debate being to define the relation of the son to the Father. The church of Alexandria was the most powerful of all the churches at this period, and it was ruled by Trinitarian bishops who took part in all these discussions. One of the most prominent candidates for the office of bishop was Arius, the celebrated originator of the

Arian doctrines and a Presbyter of the Alexandrian church. He and his followers maintained, in opposition to the other bishops, that the son of God was merely a creature or a created being, that there was a time when he did not exist. He said: "If the Father begat the Son, he that was begotten had a beginning in existence; from this it is evident that there was a time when the Son was not in being, it therefore follows that he had his existence from nothing." This argument was the strongest of all the blows which were given to the Trinitarian doctrine, as well as the most potent against the divinity of Jesus the Christ, because it evidently denied the co-eternity of the Father and the Son by proving the subordination of the Son to the Father, and, in consequence, inequality between them. It also indirectly implied that there was a time when the blessed Trinity did not exist.

The question was vehemently discussed again and again in public debates by bishops and Christians, and gradually the strife spread so far that the Jews and pagans amused themselves by giving theatrical representations of the contest on the stage, the point of their burlesques being the equality of the age of the father and son. The violence of the controversy at last reached the point where imperial force was needed for the decision. Emperor Constantine, being referred to, summoned the council of Nicea in 327 A.D. and settled the dispute of the bishops by formulating the famous Nicean creed and attaching to it the anathema: "The holy Catholic and Apostolic Church anathematizes those who say that there was a time when the Son of God was not, that before he was begotten, he was not, and that he was made out of nothing or out of another substance or essence and is created or changeable or alterable."

In this manner the so-called satisfactory solution of that most bewildering problem of the divine incarnation of Jesus was arrived at, and it was accepted, not because of the unanimous opinion of all the members of the council, but simply because the majority of the bishops were in favor of it. After this decision Arius was excommunicated for his heretical ideas, while his followers, who were quite numerous, were cruelly persecuted and their writings destroyed. Since that time the bishops and clergy have been forced to accept the doctrine of the Trinity as also that of the incarnation of Jesus of Nazareth.

Although the question of the incarnation of the omnipresent, omnipotent and omniscient heavenly Father in human form was thus apparently solved by the church and theologians, still it has not ceased to rise again and again in the thoughtful minds of different people in different countries, disturbing their peace and frequently driving them into agnostic and atheistic beliefs. Many a soul has often cried aloud in despair: "What a revolting absurdity it is to think that the infinite and almighty Creator and Ruler of the infinite universe should be born in a manger, should suffer from hunger and thirst, should be tempted by the devil, chastised and scourged by ordinary mortals and forced to ignominious death upon the cross!" Devout Christians do not dare to see this absurdity or to express their opinion for fear of blasphemy and punishment; but truth-seeking, rational minds cannot rest content with mere doctrines and dogmas based upon the quicksand of the authority of some book or person.

The question presents itself: "Is there any other way of understanding what is meant by an incarnation of God?" Outside of the Christian religion, there is one other religion or religious philosophy—that of Vedanta—which explains through reason and logic the problem of divine incarnation in human form upon this earth. India is the only country where the origin of this idea can be traced back and where the belief has prevailed from prehistoric times. Long before Jesus of Nazareth was recognized as the incarnation of divinity, the Hindus had a clear conception of this idea. Volumes upon volumes have been written in Sanskrit describing why and how the Supreme Being manifests Itself in human form at different times among different nations.

One of the principal points in which the Hindus differ from the Christians is in maintaining that, if God incarnates or expresses His divinity in human form, His incarnation cannot be limited by time, place or nationality. The Hindus believe that there were many incarnations before and have been many since the advent of Christ, and that all these incarnations of God are equal in greatness, majesty, wisdom and divine powers, especially in the power of saving mankind by setting forth the highest ideal of life and by leading men from the path of unrighteousness to the ultimate goal of all religions. Who could have understood and realized the highest aim and purpose of human existence, who could have solved the most bewildering questions and problems concerning the true nature and destiny of human souls, if God himself had not revealed these things to mankind from time immemorial? Could ordinary human beings with their short-sighted intellect and imperfect understanding, living constantly on the animal plane of the senses, deluded by the phantoms of phenomenal appearances and always mistaking the unreal for the real, have ever discovered the ultimate purpose of life and the true nature and destiny of human souls? Think of the innumerable opinions of atheists and agnostics, materialists and thinkers of different capacities which have bewildered the intellect and understanding of the vast majority of people!

All true knowledge is but the expression of divine wisdom. All the powers that make one great, spiritual, righteous and wise, are only the divine powers manifesting through human forms. Therefore it is said in Vedanta: "All that is glorious, grand, extremely righteous or spiritual, is the outcome of the powers which proceed from the infinite source of all forces and of all energy in nature. Wherever there is anything that is extraordinary or unusually uplifting to the soul, there is a special expression of the divine power."

According to the religion of Vedanta, the incarnation of God means the embodiment of divine qualities and divine powers. It takes place whenever and wherever such a manifestation is necessary. The blessed Lord Krishna, one of the great incarnations of divinity, who appeared about fourteen hundred years before the birth of Christ, in speaking of divine incarnations, said:

"Wherever true religion declines and irreligion prevails and whenever the vast majority of mankind, forgetting the highest ideal of life, travel on the path of unrighteousness which leads to the bottomless abyss of ignorance, misery and sorrow, the Supreme Being manifests His divine powers to establish righteousness and true spirituality by assuming a human form and living in our midst, but at the same time showing to all that He is the real master of nature and absolutely free from all the bondages of the world and its laws."

Such embodiments may take place at any time in any country. The Hindus believe that there have been many such incarnations of divinity in the past and that there will be many in the future. Krishna, Buddha, Jesus the Christ, Chaitanya, Râmakrishna, each one of these has been considered to be the embodiment of divine qualities and divine powers. The lives and deeds of all of them were superhuman, consequently divine. They were full of the manifestations of such powers as ordinary mortals do not possess.

A divine incarnation is one who shows from childhood that he is a born master of mind, body and senses, and the real Lord of nature, yet who never forgets even for a moment that he has come to the world to help mankind. He is always conscious of his divine power and he manifests divine glory through every action of his daily life. He never loses consciousness of his oneness with the eternal Truth, or the Father of the universe, the infinite source of wisdom and intelligence. He lives in the world like an embodied soul, possessing perfect peace, tranquillity, happiness and blissfulness, without depending upon the conditions and environments which apparently bind the souls of ordinary mortals.

The difference between an ordinary human being and an incarnation of God lies in the fact that the individual soul of a common man takes birth subject to the laws of *Karma*, or the laws of causation and of action and reaction, in order to reap the results of the works of his previous births and to fulfil the desires that are latent in him; while a divine incarnation is the embodiment of his own free will, which alone governs him. Being absolutely free he is not forced by the law of Karma or any other law to take a human body, nor does he wish to fulfil any of those desires that proceed from the selfish nature of ordinary mortals. His soul is not subject to the law of evolution like that of any other being. He is absolutely perfect from the very moment that he assumes human form through the inscrutable power of his own omnipotent, supreme will or Mâyâ. Although such an incarnation of God is beyond birth and death, he still apparently submits, for the time being, to the conditions of the human plane, and obeys the laws that govern that plane; yet at the same time he makes people realize that he is the master of nature, not its slave, and that in reality he does not obey its laws but that the laws of nature obey his omnipotent will. Ordinary people, whose spiritual eyes are not open, may not see the difference that exists between his actions and those of a common mortal and may treat him like an ordinary man; but those who are highly advanced in spirituality, who understand the true nature of the individual soul and of God and of their mutual relation, see the difference at once, recognize his divinity and worship him as the ideal embodiment of divine powers and divine qualities.

It is for this reason that the blessed Lord Krishna, the Hindu Christ, says in the Bhagavad Gitâ: "People who are deluded by my mysterious power of Mâyâ, do not know Me as unborn and unchanging; I am not manifest to them. The unintelligent regard Me in the light of an ordinary being with a material form which is the result of past actions, and know not that I assume at will glorious and holy forms for the protection of the world."

The religion of Vedanta teaches that such incarnations of Divinity are not limited by distinctions of sex; they may appear in masculine or in feminine form according to the needs of the time and place. To the sexless Supreme Being who is both the Father and Mother of the Universe, the masculine and the feminine form are of equal value and importance. It is for this reason that amongst the Hindus in India are to be found many incarnations of Divinity in the form of woman.

The latest divine incarnation was one who appeared in the middle of the nineteenth century. He lived near Calcutta and his name was Râmakrishna. He is to-day worshipped by thousands of educated Hindus just in the same way as Jesus the Christ is adored and worshipped in Christendom. From his childhood he showed his divine power and set an example of absolute purity and divine spirituality, like an embodiment of those blessed qualities which adorned the characters of previous incarnations, such as Krishna, Buddha, or Jesus the Christ. Those who had the good fortune to see and be with him even for a short time, had their eyes opened to the truth that he was absolutely superhuman. Although he had received no school education, his wisdom was vast. He was the storehouse, as it were, of unlimited knowledge, and he showed at every moment of his life that he was the absolute master of his mind, body and senses, that he was entirely free from all the conditions that make an ordinary mortal a slave to passions and desires. He was like the personification of the Sermon on the Mount. No one could ever find the slightest flaw in his noble and divine character.*

At one time he was asked: "What is the difference between a holy sage and an incarnation of God who is called the Saviour of mankind?" He answered: "A holy sage is one who has realized God through great pain, long prayers and severe penances and after much trouble has saved himself from the attractions of the world, but he has not the power to save others; while a Saviour is one who can easily save hundreds without losing his own spirituality. A holy sage may be compared to a reed floating in the ocean of

* Those who wish to know more about the life of this divine man and why he is worshipped as a Saviour of mankind, may read Swami Vivekananda's lecture on "My Master," or "Life and Sayings of Râmakrishna," by Prof. Max Müller.

life, which cannot bear the weight of even a crow, but when a Saviour descends He easily carries thousands across the ocean like a large, powerful steamer which moves swiftly over the waters towing rafts and barges in its wake. The Saviour, like the most powerful locomotive, not only reaches the destination himself, but at the same time draws with him loads of passengers eager to go to the abode eternal of Truth."

Such is the power and strength of an incarnation of God. An ordinary person may strive and after a long struggle may attain to the realization of truth which is salvation, but with a Saviour, this is not the way; he comes to help and save others. Whosoever worships and is devoted to any of these Saviours will, through that power of devotion alone, reach the ultimate goal of all religions. As Jesus the Christ said: "Come unto me all ye that labor and are heavy laden, and I will give you rest," so the other incarnations of Divinity like Râmakrishna, Buddha and

Krishna spoke to their followers, saying in the words of Krishna:

"Giving up all the formalities of religion, come unto me, take refuge in me and I will give thee rest and make thee free from sins; grieve not, I will also give thee eternal peace and everlasting happiness."

Son of God.

"*The Divine Lord says: 'A portion of Myself hath become the living Soul in the world of life from time without beginning.'*"—Bhagavad Gita, xv, 7.

Son of God.

It is a general belief among Christians that nearly two thousand years ago the only begotten Son of God descended upon this earth to save the souls of sinners from eternal perdition. Thoughtful people, however, may wish to enquire into the true significance of this expression "Son of God." Again and again are asked the questions: "Why should Jesus the Christ alone be called the only begotten son of God?" "In what sense was he the son of the heavenly Father?" "Is not every individual a child of the heavenly Father when it is said in the 14th chapter of Deuteronomy, 'Ye are the children of the Lord your God;' or when Moses said, 'Is not he thy father that hath bought thee, hath he not made thee and established thee?'"

(Deut. xxxii, 6.) And the Hindu asks: "Why should we not recognize the divine sonship in Krishna, Buddha, Râmakrishna and in other Saviours of the world?"

All these and similar questions disturb the minds of those who are not satisfied with the sectarian explanations regarding the sonship of Jesus the Christ which they have been hearing over and over again from their childhood. Of course we have nothing to say to those whose minds are contented with such explanations, or who believe in the literal meaning of the passages descriptive of the supernatural birth and miraculous deeds of the only begotten son of God. But there are many who do not believe in miracles, who do not accept anything upon hearsay or because it has been written in a certain book or been declared by a certain great personage. They wish to go to the very bottom of things before they accept them as true; they want to know in what sense the divine sonship of the heavenly Father was understood by Jesus of Nazareth and his direct disciples.

It is extremely difficult for any one to know exactly what Jesus meant by his sonship since he has left no writings of his own. We can only gather some idea from the interpretations of his followers and from the writers of the four authentic gospels. After studying carefully the synoptic gospels we learn that there were among the authors of these books two conceptions of the son of God. Matthew and Luke accepted Jesus the Christ as the only begotten son of God because of his supernatural birth, which was caused by the inscrutable power of the heavenly Father. According to these two Gospels it was a miracle; and upon this miraculous conception of Mary and the supernatural birth of Jesus depends the popular meaning of the divine sonship of Jesus the Christ. All the orthodox sects and denominations of Christianity, accepting the miracles described in Matthew and Luke as literally true, give this miraculous birth as the reason why Jesus alone should be called the only begotten son of God. They do not recognize that other Saviours of the world, like Buddha and Krishna, had a similar supernatural birth and that their deeds were as miraculous as those of Jesus the Christ. If we ignore them, it will be quite easy for us to accept Jesus the Christ as the only begotten son of God.

The other conception of the son of God which we find in the fourth gospel, has a very deep philosophical significance. Before we discuss this point, let us understand clearly what conception of God the Jews had both before and after the time of Jesus the Christ. We know that the Jewish idea of God was at that time purely monotheistic. The God of Judaism was the creator and governor of the universe; He dwelt in a heaven far above mundane existence; He was so high and separate from the world, so extra-cosmic, so great, so majestic and so transcendent, that no one could approach Him, no one could live after seeing Him face to face. Consequently there was a wide gulf of separation between God and man, between the creator in heaven and the creature on earth. The idea of divinity in man was unknown to the Jews; such an idea would have been considered blasphemous by them. The Jews could never believe that Yahveh would stoop so low as to come down on the human plane or to live in a human form. The same spirit prevails among the Jews of to-day, and it has also been inherited by the Mahometans. According to them God is far above man, no human being can ever represent His divinity, and there can be no other relation between man and God, between the creature and his creator, than that of a servant to the all-powerful master, or that of a subject to the most tyrannical monarch. The passages that have been quoted from the Old Testament like, "Ye are the children of God," meant nothing more than the fatherly goodness of the Creator and the implicit obedience of the creature, as that of a dutiful son to his father. They were never meant in the sense in which the Christians understand the divine sonship of Jesus the Christ. Through the paternal goodness of Yahveh, Abraham became the friend of God and Adam became the son of God, as described in the thirty-eighth verse of the third chapter of Luke.

Nearly two centuries before the advent of Jesus the Christ, when the Jews came in contact with the Greeks, they found in Greek mythology a belief in Zeus-pitar or Jupiter, who was conceived as the Supreme Deity and the creator of the universe. He was not only the father of the gods and of the whole world, but also the father of the most powerful kings and heroes, who were called the children or the "offspring of Zeus" in the literal sense of these terms. We all know that the gods of Greek mythology could marry mortal women of virtuous character and could beget children, while mortal men were allowed to marry goddesses. Æacus, for instance, was born of Ægina but his father was Zeus the Supreme Deity; while Achilles was the son of the goddess Thetis by a mortal father named Peleus.

These ideas, however, were not acceptable to the Jews; on the contrary, they were considered as blasphemous and were rejected by the orthodox Hebrews. History nevertheless tells us that the worship of Zeus-pitar or Jupiter was introduced into Babylon and Northern Palestine by Antiochus Epiphanes between 175 and 163 B.C. The orthodox Jews revolted against this innovation; still there were many liberal-minded Jews among the Pharisees who liked the idea, accepted it and preached it. Among these was Rabbi Hillel, one of the most prominent of Jewish priests of that epoch, who lived a few years before Christ and died when Jesus was ten years of age. He was considered by many scholars as the true master and predecessor of Jesus and was held in great esteem by the Pharisaic sect of the Jews. He inculcated the belief in the merciful and fatherly character of Yahveh like that of Zeus-pitar, and it was he also who introduced the golden rule for the first time. At the same moment Philo and the Neo-Platonist Jews in Alexandria were teaching the fatherly character of Yahveh and the only begotten sonship of the Greek Logos or the Word. Philo was a contemporary of Jesus, but he never even mentioned his name. Many of the Oriental scholars and higher critics of the New Testament say that the writer of the Fourth Gospel must have been a follower of Philo, because in this gospel alone Jesus the Christ is identified with the Greek Logos, which was explained by Philo as the only begotten Son of the Almighty Heavenly Father.

Some people claim that the Messianic hope of the Jewish prophets was fulfilled in the personality and character of Jesus and that for this reason he was called the Son of God; but critical readers of Jewish history know perfectly well that the Jewish conception of a

Messiah had nothing to do with the Christian idea of the divine sonship of Jesus the Christ. History explains to us the social and political conditions of those days which gave rise to the Messianic conception of a deliverer from the sea of misfortune in which the Jewish nation was well-nigh drowned. For centuries the Jews had been conquered and subdued by the Persians, Greeks and other stronger powers around them. Social intrigues, political insurrections, rebellions, and constant wars raged in almost every community and kept the people busy for many years before, during, and after the time of the Babylonian captivity. Such a period naturally kindles the fire of patriotism in the hearts of a nation and forces its members to be active in every possible way. The misfortunes and calamities which befell the descendants of Israel made them remember the promises of Yahveh, which had been handed down to them through the writings of the prophets, and compelled them to seek supernatural aid for the fulfillment of those promises.

The unconquerable pride of the sons of Israel which made them feel that they were the chosen people of Yahveh, the only true God, who was their director and governor, stimulated their minds with the hope that through the supernatural power of Yahveh the kingdom of their ancestors would be restored, that a member of David's house would appear as the Messiah (the Anointed), and sit on their throne, unite the twelve tribes of Israel under his sceptre and govern them in peace and prosperity. This was the first conception of a Messiah that ever arose in the minds of the Jews. It was the principal theme of the Jewish poets and prophets who lived during the Babylonian exile. The glory of the house of Israel and the earthly prosperity of the worshippers of Yahveh were the highest ideals of the Jews. They did not mean by Messiah a spiritual saviour of sinners from eternal perdition, for they did not believe in eternal life of any kind.

The Christian idea of a Messiah as the Saviour of the world and a deliverer from sin and evil does not owe its origin to the Messianic hope of the Jews but to the Persian conception of the coming of *Sosiosh*, who, according to the promise of Ahura Mazda, would appear in the heavens on the Day of Judgment, destroy the evil influence of Ahriman and renovate the world. Some of the Pharisees accepted this idea. Most probably Jesus of Nazareth was familiar with this Persian conception of the Messiah, but at the same time he tried to spiritualize the Jewish ideal by preaching a reign of righteousness and justice, instead of a reign of war and strife between nations, a kingdom of peace and love instead of a dominion of earthly power and prosperity.

Thus we see why the Messianic hope of the Jewish prophets was not literally fulfilled in Jesus the Christ, and why the conception of a Messiah does not explain the true meaning of the Christian idea of the divine sonship of Christ. We have already seen how the Judaic conception of God made Yahveh extra-cosmic and unapproachable by human beings, and how a vast gulf of separation was thus created between God and man, between the Creator and his creatures. Many of the prophets felt it strongly, especially when Judaism came in touch with the Hellenic religion which made God so near and approachable to mortals. Various attempts were made to bridge over this gulf of separation between man and God, between the visible and the invisible; and these attempts eventually resulted in the acceptance of the Logos theory of the Greek philosophers by the Alexandrian Jews, who, as I have already said, lived about the time of Jesus the Christ. The foremost of them was Philo. It was he who first succeeded in showing the connection between the visible world and the invisible creator through the Logos of the Stoics and Neo-Platonists; but at the same time he gave a new interpretation to this word.

"Logos" is a Greek term meaning originally "word," not in the sense of mere sound, but also of thought embodied in sound—as when we utter a word, the meaning is included in the sound, since words are nothing but the outward expressions of thoughts which are imperceptible. From the time of Heraclitus, the most ancient Greek philosopher, down to the time of the Neo-Platonists this term was used by different thinkers in various senses. According to Heraclitus, Logos meant fire, which was conceived as the all-pervading essence of the universe out of which emanated the individual soul of man. Anaxagoras understood by Logos the cosmic mind, a portion of which was manifested in the human soul; but the Stoic philosophers who came later, meant by it reason or supreme intelligence. Logos pervaded all matter, and reason or intelligence in man was considered to be a part of the universal reason or intelligence or Logos, through which was established the connection between man and the Divine Mind. In fact Logos always signified the nexus between the manifested world and its Cause.

As has already been said, Philo, being brought up in the Neo-Platonic school, adopted this Stoic theory of Logos to explain the relation between Yahveh, the Supreme Creator of the Semitic religion, and the visible mortal man of this world. But he meant by Logos the ideal creation which existed in the Divine Mind before the actual creation. For instance, before the creation of light God said, "Let there be light." These words, however, were merely an audible expression of the thought or idea of light that existed in the Divine Mind: the creation of the external light was therefore nothing but the projection or expression of the idea or thought of light in the Divine Mind. As this ideal light may be called the connecting link between the gross visible light and the invisible Divine Mind, so the ideal creation becomes the bridge that spans the gulf of separation between the invisible creator and the gross phenomenal creation, and this idea or thought of the Divine Mind was the Logos of Philo;

it signified the universal thought of the world or the ideal world in the mind of the Divine Being before anything came into existence. Like a dream, the world of ideas appeared in the Divine Mind and was afterwards projected in physical space, just as a carpenter, before he makes a chair, forms a mental image of it and then projects it outside. Since this Logos or the ideal world was the first emanation or expression of the cosmic mind, it was called the "first born," "the only begotten son," "the unique son;" all these terms, however, were used by Philo and his followers in their poetical or metaphorical sense. According to this theory, the universal Logos included all the ideas and thoughts, or rather the perfect types of all created things that exist in the universe. Before a horse was created, there was a perfect idea or type of horse in the Divine Mind. We do not see this perfect type in the world; we may see a red or a black horse, a large or a small horse, but we cannot see the ideal horse. What we call a perfect horse is nothing but the nearest approach to the perfect ideal horse that exists eternally in the Divine Mind. So it is with every created species, thing or being. Before man came into existence there was an ideal man or a perfect type of man in the thought of God, and its projection or physical manifestation became something like that ideal type, because the gross manifestation, being limited by time, space, and causation, cannot be exactly the same as the ideal type which is perfect.

This ideal, or the perfect type of man, which existed in the Divine Mind, is eternal and a part of the universal Logos. All human beings, therefore, are more or less imperfect expressions of that ideal man or Logos or the first begotten son of the Divine Mind. It does not refer to the human form alone, but also to the perfect character or the soul. The individual souls, however perfect or imperfect they may be in the actions of their daily life, are potentially the same as the Logos, or the universal ideal man that existed in God's mind before creation. Every one of us is trying to express as perfectly as possible that ideal type of man in whose cast we have been moulded by the divine hand. Each one of us, therefore, is one with that first begotten son of God—such was the original meaning of the "Son of God" according to Philo and his disciples. We must not forget, however, that Philo did not know Jesus the Christ, although he lived at the same time. The writer of the Fourth Gospel, whoever he may have been, was an advocate of the Logos theory of Philo as well as a believer in Christ as the perfect type of man or the incarnate word of God on earth in the truest sense of the term. It was for this reason that he began the gospel with that famous verse, which has created so much confusion in the minds of Christian theologians: "In the beginning was the Word and the Word was with God, and the Word was God." The meaning of this passage will be clear if we remember that the author of the fourth gospel identified the Word or Logos of Philo with Christ—but not with Jesus of Nazareth, the son of Mary—and that since then this Christ has become the only begotten Son of God.

Furthermore, it should be understood that the word "Christ," like the word "Logos" of Philo, did not at first mean any particular individual or personality, but it referred to the universal ideal type of man, or the perfect man who dwells in the Divine Mind from eternity to eternity. In this sense the word Christ is as universal as the Logos. It is not confined to any particular person or nationality. We must not confound this ideal impersonal Christ or the only begotten Son of God with the historical personality of Jesus of Nazareth, the son of Mary; but we must take it in its true spiritual sense, we must understand that each individual soul, being the expression of the first born Son of God, is potentially the same as the only begotten Son of God, or the child of Immortal Bliss as it is said in Vedanta. When we have realized this impersonal ideal Christ in our souls, from that very moment we have become Christ-like; and it is then that the impersonal Christ, the only begotten son, will be born within us.

Very few of the true Christians can fully understand this most sublime universal meaning of the divine sonship of Christ and consequently of every living soul. It is extremely difficult for them to extricate their minds from the maze of the traditional personality of Jesus of Nazāreth. Students of Vedanta, on the contrary, can comprehend this universal meaning very easily, because in Vedanta the question of the historical personality of an individual, however great and spiritual he may be, is not the principal point to be discussed; its sole aim is to lift us above all limitations of personality and to lead us to the realization of the universal Truth or the Divine sonship of each individual soul. We are all children of Immortal Bliss, of the omnipotent and omniscient Divine Being. We are not children of some other being, nor are we children of earthly fathers. Parents have not created our souls, but on the contrary our souls existed even before the creation of the world. By our birthright, as it were, we possess the claim of divine sonship. No one can deprive us of this right. We may think of ourselves at present as mortals subject to birth and death, to grief, sorrow, and misery; we may call ourselves sons and daughters of men, but the time is sure to come when our spiritual eyes will be opened to the truth of our being as sons of the Heavenly Father.

The expression "Son of God" shows in a metaphorical way the extrinsic variety and the intrinsic unity that exist between the soul of man and the Supreme Spirit. Outwardly the child is different from the father, but his whole soul is one with the father. If we can leave out the external and go to the innermost depth of our souls, there we shall see and realize our divine relation, and eventually we shall become one with the Supreme Spirit and say, as did Jesus of Nazareth, "I and my Father are one." We must learn that becoming means knowing and knowing is becoming. When we know ourselves as children of earthly fathers, we have become so; and when we know that we are children of God, we become such. This we shall be able to understand better from the parable of the King's son and the shepherd.

There was a very powerful king in ancient India. By his conquests he became emperor, but unfortunately in the prime of life he suddenly died and within a few months his queen passed away giving birth to his only child, the heir to the throne. The other members of the royal family, in order to usurp the throne, took the babe away, left him in a distant forest, and spread the news that the child was dead. Fortunately he was discovered by a shepherd who went into the forest for hunting. This man had no children of his own and out of compassion he took the child, brought it home, and gave it to his wife, asking her to take care of it as her own babe. The child was brought up as a shepherd boy; he did not know anything of the secret, he called the shepherd his father, played with other shepherd boys and tried his best to help his father in his work and to earn a share of his living. He felt sometimes very miserable and unhappy, but he did not know anything better.

After a few years, when he grew older, he happened to meet the old prime minister of the deceased emperor. The minister, who knew the whole secret, at once saw in the face of that young shepherd a resemblance to the emperor and, instantly recognizing him, addressed and honored him as the prince and heir to the throne. The shepherd youth looked at the minister in great amazement and could not believe his statements; but the minister persuaded him to come to the palace, made him sit on his father's throne and asked him to take care of the property and govern the empire. Gradually the mind of the young shepherd woke up, as it were, from a dream and he realized that he was the only son of the emperor, governed his empire, and became the emperor.

Even so it is with us, being children of the Emperor of the universe; we have forgotten our birthright and are acting like the shepherd boy. The moment that we know who we are and what we are, that very moment we shall become conscious of our divine heritage and shall understand that in reality we are not children of earthly parents but of the Father of the universe. No one can deprive us of this divine birthright.

All the great Saviours of the world, like Krishna, Buddha, Christ, were conscious of their divine sonship from their childhood and never forgot it. They were like the prime minister; they came to the shepherd boy of the human soul to give the message of truth, that it is not the son of the earthly shepherd father but of the Emperor of the universe. Let us enter into our divine heritage and rule our heavenly empire. Let us become like the emperor of the universe. Let us follow the paths of the great Saviours of the world, each one of whom manifested in his life the perfect type of man, the ideal man, the Word or Logos. Let us obey their instructions and, by manifesting divinity through humanity, let us become perfect even as the Father in heaven is perfect; then we shall be happy both here and hereafter and shall attain to that everlasting bliss, which is the goal of all religions.

Divine Principle in Man.

"*There is in this body a higher Soul, the Looker-on and the Sanctioner, the Sustainer and the Experiencer, the Mighty Lord, who is also designated the Supreme Spirit.*"—Bhagavad Gita xiii, 22.

"*He who is the Omniscient Knower of all, whose glory is manifested in the universe, dwells in the heart and assuming the nature of the mind, becomes the guide of the body and of the senses. The wise who understand this, realize the Self-effulgent, Immortal, and Blissful One.*"—Mundaka Upanishad ii, 2 Kh. 7.

Divine Principle in Man.

THE study of human nature is the most interesting and the most beneficial of all studies. The more we study ourselves, the better we can understand the universe, its laws, and the Truth that underlies its phenomena. It is said, "man is the epitome of the universe; whatever exists in the world is to be found in the body of man." As, on the one hand, we find in man all those tendencies and propensities which characterize the lower animals, so on the other, we see him manifesting through the actions of his life all those noble qualities that adorn the character of one whom we honor, respect and worship as the Divine Being. Human nature seems to be a most wonderful blending of that which is animal with that which is called divine. It is like the twilight before daybreak, through which the darkness of the night of the animal nature passes into the glorious sunshine of the supreme wisdom. Human nature may be called the state of transition from the animal into the divine. The animal nature includes the love of self or the attachment of one's self to one's body and to everything related to the body and the senses, desire for sense pleasures and sense enjoyments, the clinging to earthly life, fear of death and the struggle for existence. Each of these qualities or tendencies is to be found in the lower animals as well as in human beings, the difference being only in degree and not in kind.

The savage man who lives like a wild beast in a cave or under trees and does not know how to build a house or cultivate the ground, but who sustains life by depending entirely upon fruits, roots, wild berries, or upon the birds and beasts that he can trap, expresses in all the actions of his life nothing more than what we have described as animal tendencies and animal propensities. If the Darwinian theory be true, then we can easily explain why there should be so little difference between primitive man and his distant ancestor, the chimpanzee, or some other member of the anthropoid species. When, however, the same wild man becomes partially civilized by learning to cultivate the land, to raise food and cook it, to build houses and live in communities, he no longer manifests these animal tendencies in their simpler and more savage forms. He gradually adopts more artful methods to accomplish his purposes. For instance, the struggle for existence depends chiefly upon physical force among savage tribes as well as among animals, while among civilized people in civilized countries a similar result in the form of the survival of the fittest is obtained, not by the display of brute force, but by art, skill, diplomacy, policy, lying, strategy, and hypocrisy. These are the offensive and defensive weapons of the so-called "civilized man."

All the vicious qualities and wicked deeds, such as murder, theft, robbery and other crimes which are to be found in civilized communities, are nothing but the expressions of the animal tendencies of man working under the heavy pressure of the rigid laws of society, state and government. They proceed from love of self or extreme attachment to the animal nature. Being guided by these lower tendencies, man becomes extremely selfish, and does not recognize the rights or comforts of his fellow-beings. On the contrary, he does everything to satisfy the cravings of his body and senses at the expense of his neighbors. But the moment that this savage man, or the man who lives like a lower animal, begins to see the rights of others, learns to love and care for his fellow-beings in the same way that he loves his own dear self and cares for his own belongings, from that time he rises a step higher than the absolutely animal plane; he becomes truly human and gradually manifests the other qualities and tendencies that accompany this fundamental moral principle—to love one's neighbor as one's self.

Upon this foundation has been built the whole structure of ethics among all nations. The virtuous qualities such as disinterested love for humanity, mercy, justice, kindness towards others, forgiveness, self-sacrifice, all these help the animal man to expand the range of his love of self and to subdue all that proceeds from purely selfish attachment to his own body and senses. The higher we rise above the animal plane, the wider becomes the circle of self-love, and instead of being confined to the body and senses of the individual, it becomes general, covering the selves not merely of dearest relatives and nearest friends, but of neighbors, countrymen, and at last, of all humanity. Thus, the more universal our love of self becomes, the nearer we approach the Divinity, because the Divine Principle is the universal Being whose love flows equally towards all living creatures, as the sun shines equally upon the heads of the virtuous and the wicked.

Anything that is done, not with a motive confined to some particular person, community or nation, but through love for all humanity, nay with a feeling that seeks the benefit of all living creatures, is unselfish; consequently it is guided by the universal or Divine Principle. The tendency of the individual self of each man is not to remain confined within one narrow circle, but to go beyond the boundary of the circle of the animal nature, beyond human nature, and ultimately to become universal. All charitable acts and philanthropic deeds are but steps toward that one goal. Well has it been said by Ralph Waldo Emerson that "the life of man is a self-evolving circle, which from a ring imperceptibly small rushes on all sides outwards to new and larger circles, and that without end."

Indeed the self of man has the constant tendency to break down all limitations, to transcend all boundaries, and to become one with the Self of the universe. A human being cannot rest contented, cannot remain perfectly satisfied while living within the limitations of his animal nature. He may appear to be contented for a time, or he may delude himself by thinking that he is perfectly happy and satisfied under these conditions, but the moment is sure to come when, being forced from within, he will give vent to the natural tendency to expand by struggling hard to reach out from the animal self and be united with the universal Self. This tendency is inherent in the very nature of man and its expression will force him to control the lower animal desires and propensities, to become the absolute master of them, and will gradually lead him to live a moral and spiritual life.

The awakening may come at any time and under any circumstances. One may be suddenly awakened in the midst of all the comforts, luxuries and pleasures of the earthly life. No one can tell when or how such an awakening will come to the individual soul. There have been many instances in India and in other countries of this sudden awakening of the higher tendency of the soul. Buddha was suddenly awakened when he was enjoying all the pleasures and luxuries of a princely life, when his mind was deeply absorbed in every enjoyment that a human being can possibly have. This awakening, which made Buddha one of the Saviours of the world and which has made others live on this earth like embodiments of Divinity, is not the result of some animal force or some lower tendency to be found in lower animals or in those who live like slaves of passion and desire, but it is the expression of a higher power. It is not love of the body or desire of the senses, not attachment to the pleasures and comforts of the animal self; it is just the opposite. It is love for humanity which makes one forget one's self. It is not a desire to gain something for one's own comfort, but it is a desire to help mankind, to remove their grievances, their sorrows and sufferings and to make them happy. It is not a clinging to earthly existence, but on the contrary, it is the expression of the desire to sacrifice one's own life for the sake of others without having the slightest fear of death. It is not a struggle for existence or the survival of the fittest at the expense of others, but it is the cessation of all gladiatorial fights, struggles and competitions, and the attainment of peace, tranquillity and happiness. It is making the weak to survive and the strong to be kind and merciful toward those who are about to be crushed by social competition. Are not these powers and tendencies diametrically opposed to those which characterize the animal man?

These higher powers and tendencies have been manifested again and again by different individuals at different times in different countries. The religious history of the world stands as a living witness of this fact. But the question arises, how do we happen to possess these higher tendencies and higher powers? Did we inherit them from our anthropoid ancestors? No indeed, because animal nature cannot produce anything that is not entirely animal. The believers in the Darwinian theory cannot explain the origin of these super-animal or rather superhuman tendencies. Have they been super-added to our animal nature from outside by the grace of some extra-cosmic Being, as it is supposed by the dualistic and monotheistic believers of Christianity and other religions? No, such a statement cannot be supported either by reason or by scientific investigation. No one has ever succeeded in proving when and how these powers and higher tendencies were super-added to the human soul. The most rational explanation lies in the statement in the book of Genesis: "So God created man in his own image, in the image of God created He him."

Let us understand clearly the meaning of

this passage. We are familiar with the popular meaning which seems absurd when we examine it in the light of modern scientific knowledge. In the first place the creation of man out of nothing six thousand years ago does not bear the test of modern geological research and discoveries. On the contrary, we are aware of the fact that man existed in the Tertiary period, several thousand years before this Biblical creation of man was supposed to have taken place. Secondly, we know that this word "image" does not mean the physical form of man, nor does it refer to the first man Adam, who was supposed to have been the perfect image of God before the Satanic temptation, and who after the fall lost that image and became imperfect, because of which it is said that all human beings have since been born in sin. We cannot believe that all of us were born in sin and iniquity, and, having lost the Divine image within us, thus became the sons of Satan or the Devil. If man was created in the image of God, it could not possibly mean that one particular man of a particular nation at a special time possessed His image, but it was meant for all human beings, irrespective of their caste, creed or nationality.

We must remember that there are no exceptions in the laws of nature. That which we take for an exception refers to some hidden universal law or truth, whether we see or understand it or not; and that explanation is correct which harmonizes with universal law and points out universal truth. If we admit the existence of the Divine image in one man, we shall have to admit it in all human beings; otherwise it will be an exceptional case, which cannot be true. As by discovering the cause of the fall of one apple from one tree, we learn the universal law of gravitation, which explains that all apples under those circumstances will fall, so by knowing that one man was made in God's image, we understand the universal truth that all men, women and children of all countries and of all times have been made in the Divine image, whether or not they have felt it, realized it, or manifested it in their actions.

If, on the other hand, it were true that all of us were born in sin and iniquity or under Satanic influence, it would have been absolutely impossible for any man at any time to manifest any of those tendencies and powers which we call divine, and we should be unable to explain why the great sages and spiritual leaders of mankind, who flourished in India and in other countries both before and after the Christian era, could show all the Divine powers and qualities that characterized the only begotten Son of God. Their lives show that every one of them manifested divinity in the actions of their daily life. Therefore we must lay aside the mythical meaning of that scriptural passage and understand it in its universal sense. Furthermore, this universal meaning of the Divine image in man was most strongly emphasized by the great seers of Truth in India from very ancient times and centuries before the book of Genesis was written or thought of. The same universal idea is the foundation of the philosophy and religion of Vedanta.

Vedanta teaches that when we speak of a man or woman as the image of God, we do not mean his or her physical form, but we mean the individual ego or the soul. If the Divine Being or God be this universal spirit then His image cannot be the physical form of man; this does not convey any idea or meaning at all. The ego or the soul of each individual man or woman is the image of Divinity. This idea has been beautifully expressed in Vedanta: "In the cave of the heart have entered the two, the one is the eternal, absolute, real, perfect and self-effulgent like the sun, and the other, the individual ego or soul, is like its reflection, or shadow, or image. The one is like the fountain-head of the blessed qualities and the infinite source of all divine powers, while the other contains the partial reflection of those qualities and powers."

Thus according to Vedanta every individual soul, whether it be more or less animal in its thoughts and actions, possesses the Divine image and is no other than the image of the Divine Principle or Being. The Divine Being is one and universal but its reflections or images are many. As the image of the sun, falling upon the dull and unpolished surface of a piece of metal, does not properly reflect the grandeur and power of that self-luminous body, but appears dull and imperfect, so the Divine image, falling upon the dull surface of the animal nature cannot reflect all the blessed qualities, cannot manifest all the divine powers, but, on the contrary, appears animal in its tendencies and propensities. As the same image of the sun will shine forth brighter and more effulgent when the surface of the metal is polished, so the individual soul will show its brighter and more effulgent aspect and will more fully reflect the divine qualities when the heart which contains the image is polished and made free from the dirt of animal desires and animal tendencies; then and then alone, this same individual soul will begin to manifest all the blessed qualities like justice, mercy, kindness, and disinterested love for all humanity. These powers are latent in all individuals, but they will be expressed when the heart is purified. "Blessed are the pure in heart for they shall see God," said Jesus of Nazareth.

The perfect manifestation of these divine powers depends entirely upon the removal of all obstructions like desire for earthly pleasures, for the enjoyments and comforts of earthly life, attachment to the gross physical body and to the senses, which force the individual soul to remain on the animal plane. Yet however animal the expression of the nature of an ordinary man of the world may be, his soul is still the image of the Divinity which holds potentially in its bosom all divine powers and all blessed qualities. Nay, even the souls of lower animals are potentially divine, according to Vedanta. The evolution of nature is required to bring out these potential tendencies, powers and qualities into their actual or real manifestations. Climbing the ladder of the evolution of nature, each individual soul or germ of life expresses its latent powers, first through the limitations of the animal nature as animal tendencies and animal desires, and lastly as spiritual powers by rising above all limitations, by transcending the boundaries of the various circles of animal, moral and spiritual nature, and approaching the abode of the infinite Divine Principle. At that time the individual soul becomes absolutely free from the bondage of nature, enjoys the supreme Bliss which is divine, and manifests all the blessed qualities. In passing through these various stages the individual ego studies its own powers, gains experience and realizes all the powers that are lying dormant within the soul.

Many people ask the question, "Why is it necessary for the individual soul to gain experience when it is potentially divine?"

The very fact that creation, or projection, means the manifestation of the potential energy as kinetic or as actual reality, forces the soul to objectify and project the dormant activities on to the plane of consciousness; otherwise how can the soul learn its own powers when they are on the subconscious plane? Take as illustration the deep sleep state: when all the sense-powers, such as the power of walking, moving, talking, and all the mental and intellectual functions become unmanifested, do we know in that state what powers we possess? No, certainly not. We can only know their existence when they are brought out on the conscious plane, when they are awakened. Is not this awakening of the dormant powers that lie buried on the subconscious plane, the same thing as the gaining of experience?

If for a moment all the individual souls that exist in the universe should cease to manifest their dormant powers, instantly the relative existence of phenomenal activity would vanish and the whole world would go back to its primordial, undifferentiated condition of nescience, which is almost similar to the unmanifested state of deep sleep when we do not dream. Therefore each individual soul is bound to gain experience after experience in the process of this manifestation of its latent powers and potential energy. Having experienced the powers and actions of the animal nature with their results, the soul longs for higher manifestations, tries to rise above that plane, and after realizing the effects of the moral and spiritual nature, it reaches perfection. In this state the soul becomes absolutely happy and contented, and, transcending the limitations of sense-powers, self-love and selfishness, it manifests the blessed qualities in the actions of its every-day life.

This idea was illustrated by an ancient sage in India thus: "Two birds of the most beautiful plumage dwell upon the tree of life, they are bound together by the tie of closest friendship. The one sits calm, serene, contented, peaceful and happy, and constantly watches the movements of his friend like a witness; while the other bird flies and hops from branch to branch, being attracted by the sight of the sweet and inviting fruits which the tree of life bears. When he is drawn toward a fruit, he tastes it and enjoys the sensation; then he tries another which appears more attractive, but unfortunately when he tastes it, he finds it extremely bitter and does not like it. (We must remember here that the tree of life is not like an ordinary tree; it bears all kinds of fruits from the sweetest to the bitterest.) Having tried the various fruits according to his desires, the bird happens to come to one that is exceedingly bitter, and having tasted it, he suffers intensely, and unhappy and distressed, he remembers his friend, whom he had forgotten for the time being. He looks for him and at last finds him seated on the top of the tree, calm, peaceful and perfectly contented. He envies his peace, happiness and contentment and slowly approaches him. As he comes nearer and nearer, lo! he is forcibly drawn into the perfect being of that witness-like friend, for he was his reflection or image."

The bird which flies from branch to branch, which enjoys and suffers, is the individual ego or the living soul of man. The fruits of this tree of life are nothing but the results of all the good and bad acts which the ego performs; and the witness-like friend is the perfect Divine Being, whose image the individual soul is. Thus having experienced all the fruits of our good and bad deeds, when we become discontented and unhappy, we seek our true, eternal friend, admire him, aspire to attain to his peace and happiness, go nearer and nearer, and ultimately become one with him. It is then that we feel happy and contented, it is then that true peace and happiness come.

As the image or reflection of the sun cannot exist for a second independent of that self-luminous heavenly body, so the individual soul, being the image of God, cannot exist even for a moment without depending upon the Divine Principle. The individual ego owes its life, its intelligence, its intellect, mind and all other mental and physical powers to that infinite source of all powers, all knowledge, all love, and everlasting happiness. In fact the individual soul does not possess anything. All these powers and forces that we are expressing in our daily life, whether animal, moral or spiritual, do not belong to us, but proceed from that one inexhaustible source. Nor is the Divine Principle far from us; He is the soul of our soul, the life of our life, and the omnipotent essence of our being.

"The Divine Principle is smaller than the smallest and larger than the largest; it pervades the infinite space and also dwells in the minutest atom of atoms; it resides in the innermost sanctuary of the soul of every man and woman; whosoever realizes that omnipresent Divinity, whose image the individual soul is, unto him come eternal peace and perpetual bliss, unto none else, unto none else."